SCHOOLS OF SCOTLAND

BOOKS BY THE SAME AUTHOR

Schools of Europe (Bowes & Bowes)
Universities of Europe „

In preparation
Children of Europe
Governments of Europe

GEORGE HERIOT'S NEW SCHOOL PLAYGROUND WITH
EDINBURGH CASTLE IN THE BACKGROUND.

SCHOOLS OF SCOTLAND

By

ANTHONY J. C. KERR, M.A.

WITH A FOREWORD BY

GENERAL SIR PHILIP CHRISTISON Bart.

G.B.E., C.B., D.S.O., M.C., D.L., B.A. (Oxon), F.S.A. (Scot.)

WILLIAM MACLELLAN
240 HOPE STREET GLASGOW
1962

CONTENTS

APPENDICES

CONTENTS

ILLUSTRATIONS

5

1st Impression 1962

Printed at the Scottish National Press by
William MacLellan & Co. Ltd.
240 Hope Street
Glasgow
C.2.

FOREWORD

by

General Sir Philip Christison Bart, G.B.E., C.B., D.S.O., M.C., D.L., B.A. (Oxon) F.S.A. (Scot.)

Aɴᴛʜᴏɴʏ Kᴇʀʀ's new book, *Schools of Scotland* not only fills a gap in our knowledge of Scottish Education, but it is stimulating and thought-provoking.

Up to comparatively recently our system of Education in Scotland produced results that were the pride of her people and the envy of our neighbours across the border.

Yet to-day many of us have doubts whether we are maintaining this pre-eminence. Indeed it is becoming all too obvious that we are not. As a nation we are falling behind, and Mr. Kerr has done his country a fine service in analysing the position and suggesting where weaknesses may be.

The great leaders of the past, from Calgacus to King Robert the Bruce, fought to ensure that Scotland should endure for all time as a Nation and not a mere region of our island.

One does not require to be an out-and-out Nationalist to be a good Scotsman, but all good Scots are proud of their country and are determined that where we differ from England that difference shall be maintained to our advantage.

Education is one aspect in which our systems differ, and Mr. Kerr skilfully probes our strong points and our weaknesses compared with English and Continental systems.

His wide knowledge makes his comparisons of great importance and will, I am sure, give much food for thought and discussion among Education Authorities.

His suggestion that Scotland should have a Staff College for potential Directors of Education, Lecturers in Education and Headmasters, particularly commends itself to me as a past Commandant of an Army Staff College.

The forum provided thereby, the time for really deep and constructive thinking, and the guidance by the best brains available, would I feel sure do much to improve our Education system and methods.

This is a stimulating and in places provocative book. But the Scots have always thrived on being provoked.

I trust it may inspire our authorities to ensure that Scottish Education again becomes the envy of all.

THE CROFT,
MELROSE,
DECEMBER, 1961.

INTRODUCTION

The main purpose of this book is to make Scotsmen think, in a more informed way, about Education in this country. At the same time I feel that English and other readers may find some interest in a brief and not too profound description of the Scottish Educational system, and have therefore tried to provide one.

It follows from the dual purpose of *Schools of Scotland* that I have explained in some detail features of Scottish Education which most of us would take for granted, and conversely that I have said a great deal about England which would be common knowledge south of the Border.

I had originally set out to write three articles for the *Scottish Daily Mail*, and a few scripts for *Radio Free Scotland* along the lines of the synopsis which I sent to the people mentioned at the end of this Introduction, and to others. It soon appeared, however, that I could not do justice to Scottish Education and its many urgent problems within so narrow a compass: encouraged by several of the distinguished education-ists to whom I had sent my synopsis, I therefore decided to write a small book.

Scottish by name and descent, and still more by choice, I was born in Switzerland and have spent most of my life in England. Besides teaching there for six years and here for one, I have visited the schools and universities of twenty other European countries. This background, rather than any long standing knowledge of Scotland, Scotsmen or Scottish schools, constitutes my qualification for attempting such a task. It was felt by Mr. Calder, who asked me to write the *Daily Mail* articles, and subsequently by Mr. Dunnett, Editor of *The Scotsman*, and by several others, that I might bring a fresh mind and an original approach to a subject under intense discussion, and it is in this spirit that I accepted their challenge. I cannot claim to be authoritative, but I may have something worthwhile to say.

A further advantage, though some will regard it as a disqualification, is that I am not strictly speaking part of the educational machine. Fully qualified by English standards, I am regarded as an uncertificated teacher in my own country, and in principle there is no official future for me here. Consequently I am not greatly worried about the way in which my promotion prospects and in general my place within the educational system could be affected by any remarks or judgments which are not to everybody's liking.

In fact I doubt whether I have said anything particularly outrageous, but it was of some help to start out knowing that, even if I said it, my position would not be more insecure than it is in any case.

It was clearly impossible for a comparative newcomer to describe and discuss Scottish Education purely on his own fund of knowledge and ideas. I have therefore taken a great deal of advice. Over two hundred copies of my synopsis were sent out to a wide variety of people—mainly Rectors and other teachers but also including peers, M.P.'s, the Editors of most Scottish newspapers, and members of that vague amorphous entity known as "the general public"—in other words you and me on anything which does not happen to be our special interest or the source of our daily bread.

After some forty replies had come in, I followed up by corresponding further with those who had most to say and by seeing them in turn, at weekends and during the summer holidays. For comparison's sake I spent a few days in Iceland, whose special problems are in many ways similar to those of Northern Scotland and the Western Isles.

Finally the rough draft of this book was typed and copies were distributed to a number of my correspondents — three of them in London, since I also wanted to ensure that *Schools of Scotland* would serve its secondary purpose of explaining Scottish Education, in clear and concise terms, to Englishmen and others. From the rough draft and their comments the definite version took shape. It is by no means perfect, but I think it fills a gap.

I am grateful to the following among many others for information, comments, opinions and general advice:—

R. M. Barlow, Esq., M.A., Warden of Trinity College, Glenalmond.

J. B. Baxter, Esq., M.A., Director of Education, Roxburgh.

Miss Fanny L. S. Begg, B.Sc., Headmistress of Toryglen Primary School, Glasgow.

H. Bell, Esq., M.A., former Rector of Dollar Academy.

H. L. Brereton, Esq., M.A., Warden of Gordonstoun School.

Gilbert S. Bryden, Esq., M.A., Secretary-General of the E.I.S.

James Buchan, Esq., M.A., Programme Controller, Grampian Television Ltd.

D. G. Cameron, Esq., M.A., Secretary-General of the S.S.A.

A. G Campbell, Esq., M.A., Secretary-General of the S.S.T.A.

Mr. Ian Campbell, Jedburgh, who played the bagpipes while I wrote the concluding pages of this book.

A. U. Case, Esq., M.A., Headmaster of Blanerne School, Hawick.

General Sir Philip Christison, G.B.E., Bart.

Rev. Dr. I. K. Cosgrove, J.P., Glasgow.

John Davidson, Esq., M.A., Glenlivet.

W. McL. Dewar, Esq., M.A., Headmaster of George Heriot's School.

Dom Mark Dilworth, O.S.B., Headmaster of Fort Augustus Abbey School.

The Editors of *The Scotsman, Scottish Daily Mail, Jedburgh Gazette, Scottish Educational Journal,* the S.S.A. and S.S.T.A. Magazines, *School and College, Jewish Echo,* and *Scots Independent.*

Hr. Helgi Eliasson, Director of Education, Iceland.

Hubert Elliot, Esq., M.A., The School House, Ettrick Valley, Selkirk.

Hugh Fairlie, Esq., M.A., Depute Director of Education, Renfrew.

Lord Ferrier.

C. H. Fright, Esq., Headmaster, Eastry School, Kent.

A. J. S. Greig, Esq., M.A., Headmaster of Rannoch School.

Hr. Johann Hannesson, Rector, Laugarvatn Grammar School, Iceland.

The Rev. G. Hislop, St. John's Rectory, Jedburgh.

Brian Holmes, Esq., M.A., London University Institute of Education.

W. Honeyman, Esq., M.A., Rector of Lochaber High School.

Dr. Alex. Inglis, Depute Rector, Bell-Baxter High School, Cupar, Fife.

James Inglis, Esq., M.A., Principal Teacher of English, Airdrie Academy.

Hr. Bjarni Jansson, Inspector of Schools, Southern Iceland.

Robert M. Kennedy, Esq., M.A., Rector, Marr College, Troon.

Mrs. M. Kermode, Member of the Education Authority, Isle of Man.

Professor J. A. Lauwerys, University Department of Education, London.

J. F. Leedham, Esq., M.Ed., Headmaster, South Wigston Junior School, Leicester.

The Marquess of Lothian.

D. A. Macdonald, Esq., M.A., Principal Teacher of Gaelic, Bellahouston Academy, Glasgow.

James Macgregor, Esq., M.A., Jedburgh Grammar School.

The Rev. Kenneth Macrae, Free Church Manse, Stornoway.

Mrs. C. McFadden, Isle of Barra.

Dr. Douglas McIntosh, Director of Education, Fife.

Dr. R. S. McLean, Director of Education, Inverness.

Robert McPherson, Esq., M.A., Education Officer, Scottish Television Ltd.

Commander P. Matheson, former Convener of the Education Committee, Roxburgh.

Mrs. Naomi Mitchison, Carradale, Argyll.

J. Robbins, Esq., M.A., Headmaster of Castlebay J.S. School, Isle of Barra.

Sir James Robertson, sometime Rector of Aberdeen Grammar School.

Alistair M. Shanks, Esq., M.A., Strichen, Aberdeenshire.

W. G. Sproat, Esq., M.A., Headmaster of St. Mary's School, Melrose.

Dr. G. Thomson, Director of Education, Ross and Cromarty.

Dr. J. Thompson, Rector, Madras College, St. Andrews.

H. C. Wilkinson, Esq., M.A., Director of Education, Isle of Man.

B. F. A. Wilson, Esq., M.A., Headmaster, Drumlanrig St.
Cuthbert's School, Hawick.

Gordon Wilson Esq., B.L., Director of Programmes, Radio
Free Scotland.

Miss Wendy Wood, Edinburgh.

Right Hon. Arthur Woodburn, P.C., M.P., and Mrs.
Woodburn.

The opinions expressed in this book are, of course, my own,
and I accept full responsibility for them. I am in no sense the
mouthpiece of the many and distinguished people whom I have
consulted, nor do their views necessarily agree on any given
point, either with mine or with one another's, but their thinking has in various ways contributed to mine.

GLOSSARY

Since this book serves a dual purpose it is necessary to explain certain Scottish terms to Englishmen and vice versa, as well as various Continental or Scandinavian expressions.

OUTWITH = the English preposition "outside", which we only use as an adverb.

FURTH OF SCOTLAND generally means "in England" but sometimes also in other countries.

PUBLIC SCHOOL: without capitals, inverted commas or italics, means a school to which everybody's children can go, and where none, as a rule, need pay.

"PUBLIC SCHOOL" as distinct from the above means a Senior Secondary School with a 13-18 age range approximately, independently managed under a Board of Governors, and charging substantial fees.

"GRANT-AIDED" SCHOOL is a school, usually Senior Secondary, independently managed as above, but subject to the Schools (Scotland) Code. It is in receipt of grant from the Scottish Education Department. The English equivalent is a Direct Grant School.

"FEE-PAYING SCHOOL" includes the two categories above. Should properly be called a "fee-charging" school but everybody knows what a "fee-paying" school means.

SENIOR SECONDARY SCHOOL is a school taking pupils up to examinations entitling them to proceed to university. Known in England as a *Grammar School*, in German-speaking countries and in Scandinavia as a *Gymnasium*.

JUNIOR SECONDARY SCHOOL is a school taking pupils only to the age of 15 or thereabouts. It may or not have an academic side. The approximate Scandinavian equivalent is a *realskola*.

OMNIBUS SCHOOL, for the purposes of this book, is a school whose primary and secondary departments are subject to the same Rector or Headmaster, and whose secondary department includes both academic and non-academic pupils. It may also mean a school where there is no clear division between academic and non-academic sides — a *comprehensive* as distinct from a *bilateral* or *multilateral* school in England. The terms "academic", etc., are explained in Chapter III.

"TEACHERS" in Scotland, and for the purpose of this book, include all who teach. In theory they do so in England too, but the English maintain a distinction between "masters" and "teachers" as do nearly all Continentals, and as I have done in "*Schools of Europe*". It is with some reluctance that I have *not* maintained this distinction, formerly current in Scotland also, and my view is that graduates, whether teaching in primary or in secondary schools, should resume their old and honoured title.

"REMIT" = English "terms of reference".

"CONVENER" = English "Chairman".

"QUALIFYING" or "TRANSFER EXAMINATION" = the Scottish equivalent of the "*Eleven-plus*" but taken a year later. The procedure is slightly different and a higher proportion of pupils "qualify".

"ORDINARY GRADE": the new Scottish equivalent of "*Ordinary Level*" in England, or *Real-Examen* in Germany and Scandinavia (approximate).

"LOWER LEAVINGS", now obsolete, corresponded to the rare "O*" or "O/A" in England, or *Baccalauréat I* in France.

"HIGHERS" = the approximate Scottish equivalent of *Abitur* in Germany, *Student-Examen* in Sweden, and *Baccalauréat II* in France. Somewhat below "A" level but in a wider range of subjects.

"ADVANCED GRADE" if and when introduced, will be the approximate equivalent of "*A*" Level in England.

"This country" for the purposes of this book, means Scotland. "Europe" includes the British Isles and Scandinavia while "The Continent" excludes both. "Scandinavia" means Denmark, Norway, Sweden, Finland and Iceland. "Northern Europe" means the above five countries *plus* Scotland, Schleswig-Holstein and the City-State of Hamburg.

NUMBERING OF CLASSES, etc.

Scottish primary classes are numbered thus: P.I, P.II, P.III, P.IV, P.V, P.VI, P.VII. P.I are starting school, P.VII about to move on to Secondary Schools.

Secondary classes are numbered S.I to S.VI in the same manner. They may be further designated by additional letters or names (Certificate, Technical, Rural or Practical, Modified) which indicate the type of course followed by the pupils. These names, if used, are normally abbreviated, and this may cause some confusion. Thus S.II.C is a second-year form but may either belong to the Certificate stream (academic) or to the " C " stream (practical).

Independent schools make somewhat different arrangements. In Preparatory Schools the First Form are usually new boys of 8, the Fifth Form are Common Entrance candidates, the Sixth Form are Scholarship candidates, and ability, rather than age, is taken into account when placing pupils in any given form and subsequently when promoting them.

In " Public Schools " the Fifth Form are taking G.C.E. Ordinary Level, generally at 15 rather than 16. The Sixth Form are working towards "A" Level or Open Scholarships. Forms below the Fifth may have names or numbers—there is usually no First or Second Form.

CHAPTER I

History

Scotland has always been rather better provided, as regards education, than most other European countries, and this even at times when she was poor and insignificant in other respects.

As was the case in England, there was a Scottish Church long before there was a Scottish nation, and the Church ran as good a network of schools as its resources—originally somewhat limited—allowed. These schools were of three main types: cathedral or monastery schools, from which the burgh schools developed in due course, parish schools—for centuries before and after the Reformation the most important element in the system—and "song schools" or "lecture schools" giving only an elementary education in the burghs.

Time and again Scottish education has been served by the relative poverty of this country, as compared with England. Scottish feudalism, of slightly later growth, was on the whole less degrading in its incidents, because the object of our nobles was to have men to fight for them rather than villeins to till their fields. In consequence they had no objection to the village "bairns" spending two or three years at the parish school. This incidentally was also true of Northern England, in many ways more similar to Scotland than to the South, and again well covered by a network of parish and monastic schools.

In the fifteenth and early sixteenth centuries, the limited endowments of most religious communities caused their schools to fall under the control of the burghs. The Provost and Bailies appointed the master, usually but not always a clergyman, and paid him out of the Common Good. As a result education was not disrupted by the Reformation and the dissolution of the monasteries to the same extent as in England.

Again there was in the sixteenth century no large class of rich yeomen farmers or prosperous merchants such as founded Harrow, Rugby, Tonbridge and many more besides. Consequently upper and middle class education was provided, not by independent schools under trustees who could and did turn the endowments to purposes other than those which their founders had laid down — usually the education and welfare of poor children in their home town — but by schools fully under the control of the local community — schools which also educated the children of artisans and labourers and, very often, girls alongside of boys.

Some of the Scottish burghs were among the first communities in Europe to impose the duty on all of having their children educated to a satisfactory standard. This was done by Cupar in 1628, by Peebles in 1637 and by Jedburgh in 1641, and it was also quite common for the burgh authorities to prohibit the establishment of private schools, other than of a purely elementary kind —or at any rate to prohibit the teaching of Latin outwith the burgh school. Thus it became the accepted practice in Scotland that all went to school together, whatever their background and whatever their future prospects.

Scotland was also the first country to have an Education Act, that of 1496, limited though it was both in its scope and its effectiveness. This required the eldest sons and heirs of barons and substantial freeholders to be sent to grammar schools about the age of eight or nine, remain there until they had " perfect Latin " and then spent three years at the schools of " art " and " Jure " so that they might have " knowledge and understanding of the laws". What the schools of " art ' and " Jure " were is difficult to say: Dr. Strong suggests they may have been a higher type of schools within the monasteries—on the other hand it may have been intended that these young men should start on the University Course, even though they were unlikely to complete it. One must remember that in the Middle Ages, and for a long time after, the great majority of students never graduated— in many cases one went to University for the social prestige of having been there and for the opportunities of sharpening one's mind and enjoying the best years of one's life rather in order to acquire a qualification of definite professional value.

The 1496 Act was mainly intended, so it seems, to anglicise and civilize the chieftains of the Celtic West and North—the Gaelic-speaking areas then being far more extensive than at the present and including well over half the country and a very large and warlike minority of its population. James IV wanted to attach the nobility to himself through education as Louis XIV through the splendours of Versailles, and for all the difficulties which he encountered, his was the sounder principle and the more lasting success.

Exactly two hundred years later we were again first in the field, with the Act for the Settling of Schools. This was essentially a re-enactment and reinforcement of several other Acts passed in the reigns of James VI and Charles I. Its essential terms were that there should be a school provided and a schoolmaster appointed in every parish, and that the heritors (freeholders) should be responsible for both, and for payment of the schoolmaster's salary, each according to his means. The heritors could recover half the cost from their tenants. If they failed in their duties the Commissioners for Supply within each County were to find the necessary monies and then recover them by fining the heritors in proportion to their means. The 1696 Act was the first that was at the same time *general in its scope* and *enforceable in practice* at any rate where public opinion was in favour of schools and the population was neither excessively scattered nor desperately poor—in other words more or less throughout the Lowlands and in the few Highland burghs. Thereafter an increasing number of burghs and lairds made school attendance locally compulsory and *predominant* if not *general literacy* was achieved within a couple of generations.

In the same year (1696) an Act of the Swedish Riksdag made *the acquisition of literacy* compulsory in the kingdom of Sweden/ Finland, but it was up to every Swedish subject to make his own arrangements to that end. There was no obligation on anybody to set up schools (though in fact the burghs and parishes did so as in Scotland) or to send his children there—though it was obviously the most convenient way to make them literate and thus entitle them to the full rights of citizenship (illiterates could neither vote nor, in theory, be married).

The *Magna Carta* of Scottish Education, however, is undoubtedly John Knox's " Book of Discipline ", published in 1560. It laid down the main lines followed by subsequent Acts including that of 1696, but it did much more—it formulated all the distinctive principles of Scottish Education, set out a detailed scheme far in advance of anything seen until the present century, and proposed means for the support of the whole educational scheme, means that would have been fully adequate at the time, bearing in mind that schools were far cheaper to build, staff and maintain than they are today, and probably gave better value for what was spent on them, the spirit of the people being what it was.

The Reformers' principles and proposals are most effectively outlined by Dr. Alexander Morgan in his *Rise and Progress of Scottish Education* which devotes a whole chapter to them.

Firstly the principles: "As the youth must succeed us, so ought we to be careful that they have the knowledge and erudition to profit and comfort that which ought to be most dear to us, to wit the Church and Spouse of the Lord Jesus".

The Church and State which were to Knox, as to medieval Catholics, two aspects of the same Christian community, both required an educated and a godly people—an ignorant man could neither be a true member of the Reformed Kirk nor a profitable citizen of the Commonwealth.

Hence: (a) education must be available to all, compulsory for all and free for all who could not afford to pay for it.

(b) Secondary education must be available and where necessary free, and compulsory for those who could clearly benefit from it, "so that the Commonwealth may have some comfort by them". To that end the right of fathers to use their sons as unpaid labourers, or place them in gainful employment, must be restricted, and maintenance grants for senior grammar school pupils and students must be provided where necessary.

(c) The Universities must be re-organised, since on their efficiency that of the whole system, and of the Scottish Reformed Church, clearly depended.

Secondly the arrangements:— (1) A school, giving at least elementary instruction in "the first rudiments and especially in the Catechism", should be set up in every parish for children aged between six and eight. Whether it went any further, and if so how far, would depend on the qualifications of the local schoolmaster or of the Minister or lay Reader acting as such.

(2) In every burgh, and in parishes fortunate enough to obtain a suitably qualified master, there should be a grammar school where Latin would be taught to children aged between eight and twelve.

(3) A few "principle burghs" were to have a senior grammar school or College where Logic, Rhetoric and Greek, as well as Latin Literature, would be taught to the ablest youths in

the 12-16 age group. Admission was to be selective, but compulsory for those selected: inspections and examinations were to be regular and frequent, at quarterly intervals.

(4) Admission to Universities was to be upon production of a certificate of competence from the Minister and other learned persons inspecting the senior grammar schools. The old "regenting" (class teacher) system was to be abolished and each branch taught there by a specialist (this was only done progressively in the eighteenth century—Edinburgh leading the way in 1708). All were to follow a common Arts course for three years, branching off into Divinity, Medicine or Law thereafter. The colleges, which competed with each other to the detriment of academic efficiency, through the duplication of staff and the dissipation of effort, were to concentrate on one job or at the most two. Thus, at St. Andrews', one college would take the Arts Students and retain them if they went on to Medicine; Moral Philosophy and Law would be taught in another, and Divinity, following on a year's Moral Philosophy in the second college, would be taught in the third.

This part of the plan is best explained in Strong's *History of Secondary Education in Scotland,* which has a diagram of the entire system on p. 60.

The Reformers' proposals fell through because the means by which the system was to have been financed—appropriation of the entire endowments of the Catholic Church in Scotland—were not acceptable to the nobles who had already taken over that wealth and refused to disgorge it. Nevertheless the nation was the better for their having been made. The ideal had been set up on its pedestal and could not be knocked down—the Reformed Church, far more powerful here than the Anglican Church in England, had dedicated itself to educating the people and was, in the main, able to win their support. Since that time we have been far more " school-friendly " than the English and probably more so than almost anyone except the Scandinavians and the Dutch, who are our equals in this respect but nothing more. Little has been heard, in this country, of " the lower orders " or of keeping them " in their proper station."

Had the whole scheme been put into effect there is a fair chance that the Act of Union would never have been necessary, since Scotland would have gained such a tremendous intellectual start that the economic difficulties, in which she found herself just before 1707, could have been overcome and perhaps avoided altogether. Incidentally the Book of Discipline and the Act of 1696 both presupposed an independent Scotland. Had Somerset's raid of 1547 become a conquest and Scotland shared in the English *imposed* Reformation instead of carrying through a *national* and *popular* one of her own, there would have been no Book of Discipline: and it is certain that no United Kingdom Parliament would ever have passed the Act for the Settling of Schools as early as the seventeenth century. It is also possible that, without Scotland's example, England might have waited beyond 1870 for the first in her series of Education Acts. It is well that we kept our freedom as long as we did.

In one respect, however, it is fortunate that the proposals contained in the Book of Discipline remained an ideal instead of becoming law: too rigid a distinction between primary and secondary education, and between junior and senior secondary education, was thus avoided and the parish schools retained, until within living memory, the possibility of giving direct access to our four Universities. This was perhaps one of the most worth-while and interesting peculiarities of the traditional Scottish educational system and I for one regret its inevitable passing. The close connection between primary and secondary schools, which are often departments of the same institution, has generally been maintained in small and medium-sized towns and this, I am sure, is educationally sound. Nothing like it exists in Western Europe, except by way of experiment: here alone this practice is rooted in the soil.

No important Education Acts were passed between 1696 and 1872 though there was minor legislation to improve the lot of schoolmasters who were, by any standard, wretchedly paid—they earned a little more than farm labourers and rather less than the better-established servants in a large house. Scottish Education continued to develop along the lines already discernible in the seventeenth century. Its rural mainstay was the parish school, with its curriculum proverbially extending " from the alphabet to Homer."

Appointed by the heritors but approved and supervised by the local presbyters, the parish schoolmaster was virtually irremovable once settled in his post. He received a salary of 200-300 marks (about £10-15 sterling) a year, which he augmented by taking fees from those pupils who could afford to pay them and by doing a variety of parish jobs — sessions clerk almost always, precentor sometimes, and very occasionally grave-digger. In principle though by no means always he was a graduate, often a licentiate awaiting his call to the Ministry — it followed that the best schoolmasters might not stay very long, and some parishes in the eighteenth century extracted from their schoolmasters an undertaking that they were not seeking and would not seek a parish charge.

What the school was worth depended on the sort of man the heritors were fortunate enough to find or compelled to tolerate. In some cases they had to make do with a lad of sixteen, saving up to go to University or teaching in the spring and summer to support himself there in the autumn and winter. At other times they might get hold of a first-class dominie who would instil basic literacy and godliness in all and send one or two " lads o' pairts " to University year after year: the danger was that he might neglect the former and larger task for the latter and personally more rewarding. This has always been a risk inherent in " unstreamed " education and indeed in all education where pupils of widely differing abilities are gathered under one roof if not in the same classroom. The schoolmaster is by nature an academic beast: like seeks like and he almost inevitably takes a *greater* interest in those who have more in common with him, and the *greatest* interest in those who have most in common with him.

This defect, however, was not a very grave one in the circumstances of the time. Though school attendance was morally if not legally compulsory throughout the Lowlands, arrangements were fairly elastic and there was no prescribed age-range. The " bairns " who only became " children," in official usage, after 1800, attended school from the age of six, seven, sometimes eight until they had learnt all it seemed they might profitably learn there. This stage was usually reached about the age of eleven or twelve. Thereafter only those who appeared to be " university material " stayed on. There was no compulsion to stay on to a definite age or to reach a fixed point in a set curriculum each year. The master and the ablest pupils set the pace; others followed on as best they could, probably doing no worse than they would have done in a noncompetitive class whose pace had been set to theirs.

Perhaps the greatest single weakness in our educational system today is that it has not really adapted itself to compulsory schooling prolonged well beyond the achievement of basic literacy. Nobody has really worked out *in detail* and *specifying ways and means* what should be done with pupils who have learnt what they can learn, or can be persuaded to learn, in an academic way, and who must remain at school two or three years more—nor has anybody really considered who should teach them nor how they should be prepared for their task.

The burgh schools differed from the parish schools in several important ways. They were of course much larger and often employed two or more masters, each in charge of a class rather than of a subject or group of subjects. Their masters were appointed and paid by the burgh authorities, not by the heritors; and the Church, though claiming the right of supervision and enforcing subscription to the Confession of Faith, had much less day-to-day control. Since there were more pupils, and more of them could pay fees, the masters were considerably better off: as in the parish schools and in the Universities their tenure, once appointed, was *ad vitam aut culpam*. The schools were essentially secondary, with a mainly classical curriculum. They might have a primary department and Latin was taught from a much earlier age than at present—usually eight or nine. But "the rudiments" were more often implanted in a "lecture school" which another master or dame, specifically prohibited from teaching Latin, ran for private profit. These little schools, also known as "private adventure" schools, multiplied exceedingly in the nineteenth century, eventually outnumbering the official burgh and parish schools by more than three to one.

Dissatisfaction with the excessive emphasis on the classics, and with the traditional inefficiency of some burgh grammar schools, lead in the eighteenth century to the foundation of many non-classical "academies," some by private persons, others by burghs. In many instances the academy eventually swallowed up the grammar school, acquiring a classical department in the process. In other cases they combined to form a loose ungovernable federation, as at Dundee High School, which had eight "sides" each under its own quite independent master.

This could give rise to many indefensible anomalies. Pupils did not enrol in one school but in several which happened to occupy the same site, paying fees to each and taking their pick of the courses. If the English master chose to give cut-price arithmetic lessons there was nothing the Mathematics master could do about it, except to give cut-price Latin lessons at the expense of the Classics master. On the whole, however, the Academies justified their existence in three ways at least:

(1) *They broadened the curriculum* by making room for more English and for Mathematics, Science and Modern languages;

HISTORICAL

(2) As a necessary means to this end they estabished the principle of *subject teaching*. This enabled each pupil to come into contact with several masters from one of whom at least he might reasonably be expected to learn something. Class teaching is unfair to the pupil who does not get on with his class teacher, and in general narrows the possible range of expansion of his mind. It has no real place in the secondary school except for pupils who are still following a primary type of curriculum and perhaps for exceptionally able pupils who require a master of exceptional calibre (it is therefore found in the Scholarship Form of some preparatory schools though in an attenuated form—the headmaster may for instance take these pupils in English, History and Classics, leaving Mathematics and French to specialists.)

(3) They forced inefficient grammar schools to improve radically or close down.

The endowed grammar schools, following sometimes the curriculum of the academies, sometimes that of the burgh grammar schools, sometimes a combination of them, appeared in the later part of this middle period of our educational history. They are discussed, together with the English-type "Public Schools," in Chapter V, as their importance fully warrants separate treatment.

Other types of schools which appeared during this period were "side schools" and the S.P.C.K.[1] and sessional missionary schools.

Side schools functioned in widely-scattered parishes which could not be served by a single parochial school. In such parishes the heritors found the salaries of two schoolmasters but were not obliged to provide dwelling-houses for them. *Sessional schools* as their name implied, were run by the Kirk sessions of a particular town rather than by a parish minister. They were established mainly in towns which put on a rapid spurt of growth in the early stages of the Industrial Revolution. *S.P.C.K.* Schools only existed in the Highlands and Western Isles: their object was to civilize, anglicise and evangelize these regions which had remained semi-barbaric and Gaelic-speaking and had either clung to "Romanism" or relapsed into irreligion.

Unlike the "side" and "sessional" schools, and the other categories mentioned above, the S.P.C.K. schools probably did more harm than good. The cause of education would have been

---

[1] Society for the Promotion of Christian Knowledge; also known as Scottish Society for the Propagating of Christian Knowledge (S.S.P.C.K.).

advanced much faster by schools whose authorities were prepared to recognise Catholicism as the faith of the people and Gaelic as their language, in the same way as Catholicism and French were recognised in Quebec about the same time. In fact the S.P.C.K. authorities did their utmost to force the closure of Catholic schools, while they only admitted Catholic pupils on condition that they learnt the Shorter Catechism, read the Protestant Bible and attended the Protestant service. In consequence the Catholic islands had upwards of 80% illiteracy just before the passing of the 1872 Education Act, a proportion at the time unequalled anywhere else in Britain. The Catholics of Banffshire, on the other hand, were no worse off than their Protestant fellow-citizens; they had been running schools of their own for a hundred years in some places, and elsewhere attended parochial schools on week-days and their own chapel on Sundays. This was partly because they spoke English, partly because religion had for long been accepted on both sides, in practice if not in principle, as a matter of family allegiance as it was in " mixed " Swiss cantons and in Dutch municipalities.

Though the network of schools partly inherited from Catholic times, partly created by the Reformers and strengthened by the individual action of burgh and parish authorities and by the 1696 Act had rendered magnificent service, it was no longer adequate in the middle of Queen Victoria's reign. The existing apparatus could not cope with the shifts of population provoked by the Highland Clearances and the Industrial Revolution, nor with its greatly increased total consequent upon a falling deathrate. Other problems too had arisen—the conflicts between burgh and Church authorities, and within the National Church itself, following on the Disruption in 1843. By 1864 the total number of schools was actually slightly larger than it is today, but the great majority were hopelessly inadequate " adventure schools," while in many small and medium-sized burghs there was wasteful duplication through the co-existence of National and Free Church schools or of an academy and a classical grammar school. Far too much depended on the luck of the draw. Scottish schools were investigated as such by the Argyll Commission in 1864/67 and, incidentally to an investigation of English schools, by Mr. D. R. Fearon, a member of the Taunton Commission, at the same time.

The outcome was the Education Act (Scotland) of 1872 a measure in itself more satisfactory than the Act of 1870, applicable only to England and Wales, and easier to enforce, because there

were more schools and more teachers while the people as a whole
were more favourably disposed towards education—more " school-
friendly " as the Germans would say.

The 1872 Act safeguarded the secondary work done in the
parish schools—of very high standard over much of the North
East and good in many other places—work that was threatened
by the application of the Revised Code and of Payment by Results
(see Curtis, *History of Education in Great Britain;* Morgan, *Rise
and Progress of Scottish Education;* Strong, *History of Secondary
Education in Scotland*). It regulated education not only in purely
or mainly elementary schools, but in mainly secondary schools
such as existed in the burghs. The main features of the Act were
as follows:

(1) a Committee of Council on Education in Scotland, more
briefly called the Scotch Education Department, was set up as the
central authority for education in Scotland.

(2) 984 School Boards, elected triennially by owners or
occupiers of property worth £4 a year or above, were set up to
administer education in districts generally corresponding to the
parishes and burghs. They took over the powers formerly exer-
cised by the heritors, the Church and the burgh councils.

(3) Education, at school or at home, was made compulsory
for children aged between five and thirteen. This was only
achieved by the Acts of 1881 and 1891 in England.

(4) Three main types of school were recognised:
  (a) public schools (mainly or wholly elementary)
  (b) higher class public schools mainly secondary and
  encouraged to become wholly so by the creation of
  elementary schools alongside them. They were subject
  to the school boards but not financed by them.
  (c) higher class schools (independently managed day or
  boarding schools).

(5) Teachers in public elementary schools had to be certificated and to have completed a course of training. Secondary
teachers need not be certificated—it was left to the School Boards
to satisfy themselves as to their competence. School boards were
given power to " fire " as well as to " hire " — the old tenure
ad vitam aut culpam was abolished, but teachers recovered some
of their old security by the 1908 Act.

(6) Existing *burgh* and *parish* schools had to be transferred
to the School Boards but the teaching of religion under the same

27

conditions as before, was safeguarded. Other grant - earning schools *could* be transferred on the same terms.

The next great step forward was the 1908 Education (Scotland) Act. It made provision for school meals, medical examination of pupils, the supply of food and clothing at public expense where necessary, and the transport of pupils or boarding accommodation when they lived too far from school to be transported there daily.

The school leaving age was raised to 14 (16 in the case of physically or mentally retarded children, at the discretion of School Boards). Continuation classes had to be made available and attendance could be made compulsory for young people up to 17.

Important *financial* regulations were also made but these are now largely obsolete, since School Boards no longer exist and education is no longer provided for out of a separate grant.

The 1918 Act set up County and City Education Authorities, existing for that sole purpose and elected for three years by proportional representation on an adult franchise. Individual schools and small groups of schools were managed, under these authorities, by School Management Committees, but these had no power over finance, the establishment or closure of schools, or the appointment, remuneration and dismissal of teachers — in effect they were there to help rather than to decide.

The 1918 Act also restricted and regulated the part-time employment of children under 13 and provided for (a) the eventual raising of the school leaving age to 15; (b) the *compulsory* institution of part-time continuation courses.

Finally the 1918 Act made two important provisions for *religious education* which to this day are among the main points of difference between the Scottish and English education systems.[1]

(a) Religious instruction could be given as before to children whose parents did not object. This was in general, Protestant instruction based on the Authorised Version of the Bible and on the Shorter Catechism.

(b) Voluntary schools could be transferred by sale or by lease or otherwise to the Education Authority in whose area they were situated. The Authority had no right to refuse once the offer was made and terms were agreed. The existing

[1] A fuller description of these arrangements will be found in Sir James Robertson's pamphlet, "The Scottish Solution" obtainable from the Church of Scotland bookshop in Edinburgh.

staff were taken over with the school which then became a public school, managed by the Education Authority on special conditions, namely that the customary type of religious instruction, usually Catholic or Episcopalian, would continue to be given there, and that new teachers must satisfy the church authorities concerned as to their fitness on religious grounds (it does not automatically follow, for instance, that all teachers in a Catholic school must be Catholics, and some are not, but they must be persons acceptable to the parish priest and willing to respect the faith of their pupils).

These arrangements are fairly similar to those which exist in some parts of Switzerland and Germany: so is the provision which can be made where separate Catholic and Protestant public schools would be impracticable or hopelessly uneconomic to run, for both types of instruction in school time and on school premises. They have given general satisfaction except possibly in Glasgow, where they perpetuate the existence of Catholics and Protestants as quite distinct *social* communities, with a radically different ethos and background.

This settlement could be reached in Scotland and not in England for a variety of reasons, which all boil down to the fact that we are another country and another people, with a very different history and character.

Non-conformity in the English sense does not exist in Scotland, except on a very reduced scale (" Wee Frees," Plymouth Brethren) because in one sense we are all non-conformists, and in another we are all established.

The National Church here is genuinely Protestant and of popular origin whereas in England it is an imposed compromise, rejected by important minorities which together add up to a majority of those who actively practice any faith. Consequently, though Baptists and Methodists remain apart from the Church of Scotland, they have no objection to their children being taught religion on the basis of its Shorter Catechism.

The main non-conforming bodies are the Episcopal and Catholic Churches. The Episcopal Church in Scotland has a much longer history than the Methodists or Baptists in England and its members largely belong to the upper strata of society, in so far as Scottish society can be regarded as stratified. It draws some encouragement and strength from being in communion with the Church of England, and Episcopalians, though non-conforming are not non-conformists in the same sense as Methodists or Baptists in England. They lack the inferiority complexes, "anti" feeling and social radicalism which are found among many if not most English Non-Conformists: their *raison d'être* is tradition rather than revolt.

The Catholic Church is deeply entrenched in many areas, some of them quite large. In the Southern Hebrides and over much of the Western Highlands it is as genuinely "established" as the National Church elsewhere. In parts of Aberdeenshire and Banffshire and in many scattered localities, it has at least a strong minority position very similar to that of the Reformed Church in several French Departments (Ardèche, Gard, Lozère, Hautes-Alpes). It is far more "part of the landscape" than in England and, except in the ecclesiastical province of Glasgow and some "overspill" areas, it commands the allegiance of a *representative* cross-section of the population, rather than of a strange combination of aristocrats, poets, novelists and day labourers. In the Glasgow province, however, it is overwhelmingly "working class" in its membership, and includes a very large non-Scottish or at least non-local element.

This being so, a working compromise was easier to reach and remains easier to maintain, even though compromise is a more typically English than Scottish trait as a general rule. Religion has become very largely a matter of local or family allegiance: one is a Protestant because one lives in Harris or a Catholic because one lives in Barra — a Protestant because one is a Campbell or a Catholic because one is a Fraser. It is as simple as that, even though clan allegiances at least are now approximate rather than absolute. Neither side seriously expects to convert the other and the Episcopalians sit quite happily in the middle: no credit or discredit attaches to being what one is. Education must be provided for all and it is easiest to provide it in the way in which people want it.

In England, however, non-conformists are often afraid of the social "pull" of Anglicanism, and they combine with the Protestant half of the Anglican Church to resist any concessions that might make life too easy for the Catholics—bearing in mind that it is mainly Catholics and Anglo-Catholics who might benefit from the incorporation of voluntary schools within the "State" system on the same terms as in Scotland. They are quite satisfied with the existing arrangements since "Agreed Syllabus" religious instruction has to be agreed by them and consists broadly speaking of what they have in common with Anglicans, their *distinctive* tenets being imparted in their Sunday Schools. Any concession to denominational religious instruction would be essentially a concession to the Anglican Church from which they revolted and the Catholic Church to which they are bitterly hostile.

CHAPTER II

Recent History and Present Organisation

The *ad hoc* authorities set up in 1918 worked well and are
nostalgically remembered by the diminishing Old Guard of
teachers and administrators who served under them, as also by
their former members. In the main they were composed of
people with a definite interest in education—notably ministers,
doctors, and employers whose labour force included a proportion
of apprentices. Their main weakness—some would call it their
glory—was that they spent a great deal of public money. They
made their decisions, they presented their estimates, and the
county and burgh councils had to raise the money somehow.
Ratepayers did not like it, nor did the Treasury, automatically
compelled to find 60% of the estimates, once approved by the
Scottish Education Department (thus renamed in 1918).

Over the heads of the Scottish M.P.'s, who voted 27-18 against
on the Second Reading, another 20 being absent or abstaining,
the Local Government (Scotland) Act was therefore passed in
1929. It transferred the functions of the Education Authorities
to County and City Councils, thus uniting administrative and
financial responsibility.

The general opinion seems to be that this was a change for
the worse, though there might have been a strong case for compelling the Education Authorities to work within the financial
limits that the County and City Councils were prepared to allow,
and arranging for mutual representation of each set of bodies on
the other.

The main drawbacks of the present system appear to be as
follows:

(1) Education Committee work, which is quite considerable
one way and another, tends to be heaped on those who have the
time to do it, irrespective of their qualifications. Many who
would have found or made time to sit on an Education Authority

GEORGE HERIOT'S COLLEGE,
EDINBURGH.

*THE BIOLOGY ROOM
AT KIRKCALDY HIGH SCHOOL.*

are not sufficiently interested in local affairs generally to stand for County or City Councils.

(2) In some Tory-controlled counties a high proportion and sometimes a clear majority of Education Committee members have been educated outwith Scotland, or at English-type boarding schools in this country. This is not necessarily a disadvantage since Scottish public schools have much to learn from *Public Schools* in the English sense. This point is discussed at some length in Chapter V. Nevertheless their lack of personal connection with the system (since they usually send their children to English or English-type schools) undermines public confidence in them, and it might be wise to stipulate a fixed minimum proportion of members who have been educated at Scottish public or grant-aided schools, or are educating their children there.

Both the drawbacks above are obviated to some extent by the co-option of members with a definite interest in education (but not teachers serving under the Committee) who might well have been elected to an *ad hoc* authority. But the co-option system is itself open to grave abuse, where it leads to the return of a member rejected by the electorate of his burgh or parish, mainly for his real or supposed disservices to education.

(3) A problem only arising in some Labour-controlled authorities. How can one trust the administration of senior secondary schools or indeed of any schools, to people who stopped learning when they were twelve and left school at fourteen? Can one even confidently expect them to co-opt people better qualified than themselves, and to reach decisions and make appointments on mainly educational rather than political or social grounds?

This problem is likely to become more serious as a result of greater opportunities for the working class " lad o' pairts " to go right through the senior secondary school and university, and thus leave the social class into which he was born. Such opportunities always existed in this country, but more boys and girls are availing themselves of them, as grants are on a more generous scale and the need to earn as soon as possible decreases. The result, is, inevitably, the intellectual devitalisation of the working class which no longer seems able to throw up leaders comparable to Morrison, Bevin, Deakin, or Citrine (it always threw up more of them in England, where opportunities to break out by education were more restricted).

(4) The constitutional defects outlined above undermine the confidence not only of the thinking public but of serving teachers,

C

even when in fact the Committee are probably doing their best in difficult circumstances. The situation is further aggravated by the advent of the Block Grant system, an obvious temptation to authorities which are mainly concerned with saving on the rates or with holding down the council house rents paid by their supporters.

With their confidence thus undermined, teachers fail to give of their best and middle-class parents are increasingly and justifiably tempted to send their children to fee-paying schools, thus depressing the tone and the academic reputation of the public schools which they forsake.

It may be added that all these abuses and dangers are far more prevalent in England, firstly because interest in education is less general, secondly because "the uneducated" tend to be worse educated than in this country or at least have been so in the past,[1] and thirdly because there still exist a few extreme Conservatives at the other end of the social scale who *think* in terms of keeping the "lower orders" in their "proper station," even if they no longer dare to avow their intentions. The whole tradition of Scotland runs against such an attitude. There are, however, some compensating advantages, mainly on the administrative side. These advantages are most in evidence where there is a strong and respected, but not dictatorial, Director of Education in charge, to offset the "amateurism" of the Committee.

Firstly the members of the Education Committee are, in many instances, members of other important committees, notably the Finance Committee and the Conveners' Committee (the Convener belongs ex-officio to both). This cuts out a great deal of paper work and delay in finding what resources are available and whether they will be made available.

---

[1] This view was challenged by one of the English critics of my rough draft. I stand by it nevertheless. Insistence on the "three R's" has ensured that everyone, or almost everyone, had a thorough grounding. At the same time everybody or nearly everybody in Scotland has had the experience of being taught, at some stage, by university-educated men and/or women and has therefore come into contact with "culture" as well as "teaching technique".

Whether this relative superiority of the Scottish "uneducated" is still being maintained is another matter. At the present time this is probably a local or regional rather than a national matter. A *good* Secondary Modern school in England is able to put on a wider variety of courses and provide a more challenging atmosphere than any *purely* non-academic school in Scotland. On the other hand I doubt whether the smaller secondary modern schools in England are as satisfactory, even for non-academic pupils, as Scottish omnibus schools with a fine tradition and the solid backing of municipal goodwill.

Secondly, though knowing relatively little about education they probably know more about life in all its aspects than the average run of educational theorists, and collectively they know more about it than a body composed exclusively or mainly of teachers and/or other persons with a definite interest in education rather than in agriculture, industry, commerce etc.

Thirdly, because they are laymen and have no personal stake in the matter, they are more likely to work smoothly with the Director of Education, who is or should be an expert, and to take his guidance at most times, while standing up to him in the public interest if he goes too far against the feeling of the local community. They may be better placed to take painful decisions such as the closure of an excessively uneconomic school, or the rationalisation of its work and staffing (e.g. by transferring the whole or the latter years of the Certificate course to a larger and more centrally placed school).

The danger in such cases (e.g. the closure of most secondary schools in Banffshire, or the transfer of third, fourth and fifth year senior secondary pupils from Jedburgh to Hawick) is that the educational and social disadvantages may greatly outweigh the definite economic and possible educational advantages. It undermines the self-respect of the community which loses its school or part of it, and creates grave staffing problems. Thus a school with a first and second year certificate side but no more must have somebody to teach French and probably Latin, unless two-language pupils go straight to a Senior Secondary School.[1] This

---

[1] The secondary department of a small burgh omnibus school (300 primary and 300 secondary pupils approx.) may be divided into three or four " sides " viz. Academic or Certificate, Technical, Practical and Modified, or Academic, Practical and Modified.

The academic pupils in such a school will all take French and a minority, the " two-language " pupils, will also take Latin or sometimes German. In most cases they will transfer to a senior secondary school after two or possibly three years. Sometimes only those pupils aiming for " Highers " will transfer: " moderately academic " pupils will remain and leave after taking the new Ordinary Grade. This is, for instance, the arrangement now in force at Laurencekirk. In some counties two-language pupils go straight into a Senior Secondary School.

" Technical " pupils where they exist (e.g. at Jedburgh) will probably take Mathematics and Technical Drawing to a somewhat higher level than " Practical " pupils. They may transfer to a Senior Secondary School and take " O " Grade or other external examinations in some subjects. *In principle* they will go into pre-apprenticeship courses rather than straight into unskilled jobs when they leave school, but things do not necessarily work out that way.

" Modified " pupils differ from " Practical " pupils in taking all subjects at a somewhat lower level: thus they may spend some consider-

35

teacher, appointed *mainly* to teach academic subjects to academic pupils, cannot be employed full-time in that capacity. He must therefore teach something else to other pupils (which he may do inefficiently and to the detriment of his proper task) or commute between two schools of this type, or teach part-time and suffer the consequent loss of pay. Since there is in any case a shortage of qualified teachers of languages, posts of this kind are difficult to fill.

I may add that, were it not for this difficulty, I would not, as an untrained graduate, have found employment in a Scottish public school and would therefore not be in a position to write this book. But that is no justification of the system.

A further disadvantage of "rationalisation" is that, in schools with an underweight academic side, most teachers are appointed mainly to teach the academic pupils, who form 30% of the first and second years and disappear thereafter. This may be unfair to the non-academic pupils, who simply exist to fill in the time-table of persons essentially interested in academic English, History, Geography, Maths and Science as well as French and Latin which are academic by nature — and in the pupils who themselves happen to be interested in those subjects and reasonably good at them. In most cases these academic teachers do their best for their non-academic pupils but the feeling for the work, and the bond of common interest with the pupils, is markedly absent. It is perhaps in this respect that *Public Schools* in the English sense are most obviously superior to public schools as Scots and

---

able time in *English* learning how to address envelopes, while their *History* may largely consist of drawing Viking ships, etc.

The proportion of pupils in each "stream" or "side" varies from school to school and area to area—perhaps 30 per cent will be "academic" and 15 per cent "modified" with 40 per cent and 25 per cent respectively for the "technical" and "practical" classes. On the whole "modified" and "certificate" classes are kept relatively small—perhaps 25-30 pupils each where "technicals" and "practicals" have 35-40. But this again varies—sometimes one will put rather more pupils into the "technical" side to appease their parents, and the "practical" classes may then have fewer pupils than "certificate" classes, though more than the "modified".

These classes, and especially the "Modified" are apt to have their names changed every now and again. For the purposes of this book, however, I have stuck to "academic", "practical" and "modified", the difference between the last two being that the "practical" are literate but not intellectual while the "modified" are not fully literate.

In a large school there may of course be several classes in each side and in each year—thus a two-language class and two one-language classes on the academic side. But there will remain a clear distinction between pupils who take a foreign language and those who do not.

Americans understand them.   This point is further discussed in Chapter V.

On balance there is probably more to be said against the present set-up than in its favour, because so much depends on the sort of people who, in any particular area, happen to get on to education committees—on their competence, their interest, their motives and how much time and energy they can spare.   But I would not go so far as to condemn it out of hand: in any case there is one corrective at present operating; the firm and progressive outlook of the younger Directors of Education.   A good Committee is often prepared to recognise the worth of an able and resolute Director and to give him a free hand within the limits set by the County's resources.   What is certain is that *ad hoc* authorities can work—there is a good one in the Isle of Man: so can bodies mainly consisting of nominated and elected teachers —in France for instance.

Two more Acts, in 1945 and 1946, set Scottish Education on its present legal basis.   The 1945 Act embodied many features of the 1944 Act in England, with some important differences—it was not so far-reaching in its scope because the Scottish educational system, as it stood, was already more satisfactory and required modification here and there rather than a drastic overhaul.   The 1946 Act introduced no new element, but consolidated existing legislation.

Some of the more important differences between Scottish and English arrangements are these:

(1) The Scottish Education Department is relatively more powerful than the Ministry of Education.   It controls, through the Scottish Council for the Training of Teachers, the organisation and curriculum of the Colleges of Education: the teaching profession is also strongly represented on the governing bodies of these colleges—whereas teacher-training colleges in England are controlled by local authorities in the same way as grammar or secondary modern schools.[1]   It must also approve the schemes submitted by the county and city councils for the transfer of pupils

---

[1] There are in fact some administrative differences.   The English Teacher Training Colleges are in most cases the property of Local Authorities, responsible for their conduct as *residential establishments* and for the buildings themselves.   Their strictly *educational* side is under the control of the University on whose territory they happen to be: thus all teaching in the London teacher training colleges is organised by my friends at the London University Institute of Education.   In some cases the *administrative* authority is not a County or County Borough, but an Anglican or Catholic organisation.

from primary to secondary schools or departments. In England local authorities have complete discretion in this matter, except that the Ministry can veto the closure of individual schools and has done so on several occasions, thus saving grammar schools which were to have been incorporated in giant "comprehensives."

(2) Besides having some additional powers the Scottish Education Department is better placed to exercise those which it has in common with the Ministry of Education. It only has 35 local authorities and 850,000 pupils to deal with, as against 150 and over 7,000,000.

(3) The Advisory Council, which it appoints and commissions to report on particular issues, is far more active than the corresponding English and Welsh bodies and has been in the field considerably longer. It meets more often, issues more reports and attracts more public attention to its doings and its pronouncements. This is due to Scotland being a smaller country than England, with fewer people and these people being more interested in education. Wales is smaller and as "school-friendly" as Scotland, but suffers from many disadvantages—lack of separate history as a nation, absence of a recognised historical capital, distraction through a linguistic vendetta, lack of national newspapers with the same standing as *The Scotsman* or the *Glasgow Herald,* or with circulation figures comparable to those of the *Daily Record,* the *Scottish Daily Express* and the *Scottish Daily Mail.* Furthermore it has even less independence than Scotland and its Advisory Council reports to a Ministry in London, not to a Department in Cardiff.

With the addition of a strong elected element the Scottish Advisory Council could become something like the *Conseil Supérieur* in France or the *Educational Council* in Holland, taking many of the more controversial decisions (e.g. closure of schools, dismissal of headmasters) now entrusted to local authorities or the governing bodies of fee-paying schools. The English and Welsh bodies certainly could not assume such responsibilities.

(4) Arising from (1), (2) and (3), there is perhaps more uniformity in practice between the arrangements made by Scottish local authorities than exists in England, and there is certainly more unity of purpose. This will be discussed further, with similarities and differences under various headings (Aims, Content and Methods of Education etc.).

In two very important respects the Scottish Education Department enjoys, if that is the correct term, a situation unique in

Europe and probably in the civilized world. It does the work of a Ministry of Education but is not one: it is a department of a large super-ministry, the Scottish Office, with a bundle of responsibilities normally only found in the hands of the few remaining Colonial Governors. At the same time, though it manages the educational affairs of what is generally agreed to be a country, not a province or a region, it is finally answerable not to the Parliament of that country, which has none, but to a supra-national Parliament, manifestly dominated by the representatives of another nation. Generally speaking, wherever there is separate responsibility for education there is a separate legislature competent to deal with it and with other matters thus decentralised. This is true of the American and Australian *States*, the Swiss *Cantons*, the German *Länder* and the Soviet *Republics*. Scotland appears to be alone in lacking such a body, even though she is more of a natural and historical entity than any of these more recent units.

There are many practical disadvantages in this set-up, as well as standing insult to our national pride, and I can see no compensating advantages.

The main disadvantages are:

(1) Whenever legislation is required, considerable delays arise because Parliament is largely preoccupied with English or British matters and has little time or interest left for Scottish business.

(ii) This legislation is discussed in detail by the Scottish Grand Committee consisting of all the Scottish M.P.'s *plus* as many non-Scots (at present about ten) as are required to maintain a Government majority.[1] It is then debated and voted on by a Parliament of 634 members, only 71 of whom represent Scottish constituencies. Some of those 71 are English, several more were educated in England—though it is true that a few Scots sit for English constituencies. Altogether between 80 and 100 members

[1] This majority must be roughly proportional to the Government's majority in the United Kingdom as a whole. It follows that if 50 of the 71 Labour M.P's were Labour, but the Conservatives had a majority of 100 in Parliament—admittedly improbable but not impossible if the English economy continued to prosper and ours to stagnate, these 50 M.P's would have to be outvoted by 68 Conservatives. If at the same time we also had 10 Liberal M.P's (not impossible in such circumstances) and five Nationalists, with perhaps a Communist or two, this would mean that 65 of the Conservative members of the Scottish Grand Committee would be Englishmen or at any rate non-Scots, and another 20 would indeed have to be added to maintain a proportional overall majority. The Scottish Grand Committee would then be 54 per cent " foreign ".

may be regarded as having reasonably strong connections with Scotland, either because they live there, or have lived there, or have to sit through meetings of the Grand Committee as silent but voting makeweights. But *all* M.P.'s may legitimately speak and vote on Scottish affairs and there is no accepted convention which prevents them from so doing. It follows that Scottish educational and other legislation may be carried through against the wishes of the Scottish people, in so far as these wishes can be ascertained.

(iii) Scotland has no Exchequer and therefore no money of her own. Part of the taxes we pay return to us in the form of Treasury Grants to the counties and to the Scottish office and its departments, for their statutory purposes. But if anything requiring additional expense has to be done, Treasury sanction must be obtained, and the Treasury cannot easily justify, to a Parliament more than 80% English, heavily disproportionate grants to Scottish authorities. It so happens that grants are slightly weighted in Scotland's favour because the total population of Scotland, though the highest ever recorded, has decreased in proportion to that of the United Kingdom as a whole and of England, in particular.[1]

But Scottish Education is proportionately more expensive to maintain than Anglo-Welsh education, for a variety of reasons. The population is more scattered and a greater number of uneconomically small schools must be kept in being or transport provided if they are closed down. The age of transfer to secondary schools is a year later: teachers in primary schools must therefore be better qualified. Twice as many pupils start on " academic " courses and more teachers of high calibre are required for them. Last but not least we are more " school-friendly " and have always tried to maintain higher standards than our neighbours and to pay our teachers more.

---

[1] These grants are calculated according to the Goschen Formula, which presupposes not that Scotland is 11/80ths of *Britain* (as commonly supposed) but that it is 11/80ths of England plus Wales, i.e. that there are 11 Scotsmen to 75 Englishmen plus 5 Welshmen. At the present time the proportion is about 11-90, but Scotland is relatively more expensive to run, as essential facilities have to be maintained in areas with a very scattered population, which contribute little in the way of rates. But far more money goes out in tax, excise, National Savings, etc. than ever comes back. The *net* loss is difficult to calculate: estimates vary from £150,000,000 to three or four times that figure. It should be borne in mind that money spent on " British " purposes (Armaments, Central Govt. expenditure, etc.) mostly remains in England, and continues to fertilise the English economy, not ours.

It seems clear that a Scottish Parliament with control over taxation as well as education would choose to spend more on Scottish Education than the Treasury is willing to allow us. Furthermore one would know at once whether or not the money was there and whether Parliament was prepared to make it available, by supplementary estimates if need be.

Not only am I unable to see any compensating advantages but I have been scarcely able to find *anyone* prepared to *defend* the existing set-up — and the names given at the end of the Introduction represent between them a very fair cross-section of educated Scottish opinion.

Fully 80% of those who expressed any views on the subject were in favour of a Scottish Government (including an Exchequer and a Ministry of Education) responsible to a Scottish Parliament. There was considerable disagreement as to what the powers of this Government and Parliament should be, but they would certainly include control over education, without reference to Westminster.

The general tendency of Scottish opinion seems to be in favour of something like the Ulster legislature and government, with perhaps rather more power; the nearest equivalent would probably be the constitutional position of an American *State* or a West German *Land*.

A minority of uncertain size demands a complete break, Scotland being connected with England only to the same extent as Norway is with Denmark and Sweden. Another minority, probably smaller among the educated but larger among the working class, supports complete integration under Westminster. This would mean the end of Scottish Education as a distinctive system, of the Scottish Education Department as a separate institution, and of Scotland and the Scottish nation as recognisable if not fully recognised entities. Only one of my " names " took this standpoint and since he has never avowed those views in public and may have changed them by now, I will spare him the embarrassment of being identified.

While only two people were prepared to *defend* the existing set-up there were quite a few who were ready to *tolerate* it as the lesser of several possible evils, and they represent the balance of my " names," apart from the lone " integrationist." It keeps Scotland in being as a recognised " country " without letting her go " on the rocks " as she might if her Parliament were permanently dominated by Socialists of a particularly irresponsible and radical brand. To ensure this did *not* happen it would be necessary to weight our Parliament, in favour of the counties and small burghs: several schemes have been proposed for doing this, all of which would naturally be inacceptable to Socialists living in the Forth/Clyde industrial belt. My own view is that we should have to adopt something like the Austrian system— permanent representation of the main parties in the Government, on the basis of their strength in Parliament at the time. Opposition and criticism would then be provided by the back-benchers. But this book is about Scottish Education, not about ways to reform the Constitution.

I must point out however that the minority who reluctantly tolerate the present set-up are *not* moderate "integrationists": they are people who would like a Scottish Parliament but fear it would not work, either because it would fall permanently under Socialist control and would so bankrupt the country, or because Scotsmen are by nature too inclined to stick up for their principles and too unwilling to compromise.[1] This brings the consensus of *educated* public opinion, such as I have been able to ascertain, to well above 90% in favour of a Scottish legislature and a Scottish government responsible through it to the Scottish people as a whole, rather than to the people of Britain or of the United Kingdom. This I think is the majority one might expect, among those bothering to vote, if a nation-wide referendum were held on that issue, after a reasonably workable scheme had been produced, satisfying those who are now gravely concerned with the possible snags I have just mentioned.[2]

One must however realise that greater self-government would by no means solve all the problems which now arise through Scotland being some way from Westminster and Scotsmen being some way from the preoccupations of those who take the vital decisions and of those in whose interest these decisions are mainly taken (i.e. the people of London, the Home Counties and the Midlands, between them electing nearly half of Parliament and most of those members who happen to have marginal seats). Highlanders and Islanders form a smaller minority among Scots-men than Scotsmen among the British, and many places are much

---

[1] Here I must point out that some of the ablest Scottish M.P's are Socialists. I am not asserting or denying the validity of this particular argument, but merely stating that it exists and is commonly used by those who are opposed to further decentralisation.

[2] It is in fact proposed to hold such a plebiscite in the near future. Details from the Hon. Sec. Scottish Plebiscite Society, Kirkton House, Forfar.

further away from Edinburgh, in time if not in miles, than the south of Scotland from London.

While there is a great and increasing weight of dissatisfaction with the constitutional set-up, many people hold that the Scottish Education Department, within the limitations imposed by its peculiar position, does the best it can and does a great deal of good, especially in channelling new ideas through its Inspectors, to schools all over the country. On the evidence available I share that opinion, but it is contradicted by others, who may be better placed to judge, and particularly by those who feel it is not doing enough to defend the Scottishness of our schools, and that it tends to absorb and pass on English ideas not on their own merits but for the sake of conformity with the rest of Britain.

The influence of the Scottish Education Department is discussed in the chapters which follow, since it is relevant to all of them at various points.

Finally a word about the basic *organisation* of our schools, whose work is more fully discussed in Chapter IV. Though the nature of primary and secondary education respectively is more clearly defined in the Scottish Education Act of 1945 than in the corresponding (English) 1944 Act, there is less of a visible break between the two. In small burghs and some larger, primary and secondary departments form part of the same school whose Rector is head of the secondary department but may find time to teach in the primary department, where he is assisted by a deputy head. He is also in constant touch with the heads of rural and housing-estate primary schools which feed his secondary department and has some sort of informal and unofficial supervision over them (in Norway and Italy at least, there exist senior headmasters with similar but statutory responsibilities). There also exist a few definitely secondary schools with fee-paying primary classes annexed to them — these classes do not necessarily follow the regular primary school curriculum, as would the primary depart-ment of a primary/secondary school: they may for instance have Latin and French. Their pupils cease to pay fees on entering the secondary department. The maintenance of these exceptional classes has been attacked as "undemocratic": its main justifi-cation is that if they were discontinued, the main school would lose valuable future pupils to a fee-paying school nearby, and its tone and academic reputation would suffer. Democracy is not served if a good public school loses all its upper-middle class pupils because it refuses to provide the sort of education their parents regard as suitable.

Transfer to secondary schools or the secondary departments of primary-secondary schools, such as the one where I taught, normally takes place when a child is twelve, and therefore after seven years in the primary school or department. English children transfer at eleven after six years, Irish children likewise, though they may only have been there five years (*compulsory* schooling starts at the age of six but the great majority enrol at five). Norwegian children transfer at fourteen after seven years: children in Communist countries do not " transfer " in our sense but normally encounter secondary subjects and teachers after five or six years and about the age of 11-12. All this is more fully explained in my earlier book " Schools of Europe " (Bowes & Bowes, 1960) and the Scottish transfer procedure is briefly described in Chapter IV of this book.

The secondary schools (including secondary departments) differ from those found in England and most other Western European countries in that fewer of them, outwith the cities and a handful of large burghs, are either wholly academic or wholly non-academic. The two most typical varieties of Scottish secondary school are the *senior secondary school*, preparing pupils for universities, but with a junior secondary side whose members leave at 15 and a technical side whose members leave at 15, 16 or 17, and the *junior secondary school* with a majority of " technical " and rural/homecraft pupils leaving at 15 (some technical pupils, however, transferring at 14 to the senior secondary school) and a substantial minority of academic or semi-academic pupils, following a senior secondary course for two years only, after which most transfer and the less able or less ambitious fall back into the technical stream. Hawick High School is a good example of the former type, being situated in a prosperous little manufacturing town with a population of about 17,000: Jedburgh Grammar School, where I taught for a year, is an equally good example of the latter in a small burgh with a population of 3,600, the centre of a landward area with another 3,500. There is no exact English equivalent to Jedburgh Grammar School:[1] in Scandinavia it would be represented by a small-burgh *realskola* such as the one at Hammerfest, near the top of the map, but with

---

[1] Bilateral Grammar/Modern schools and some of the better-staffed and more ambitious Secondary Modern Schools might be regarded as *approximate* equivalents, but would be much larger, with 600 pupils where Jedburgh has about 300 in its Secondary Department.

all or nearly all pupils learning a language (in this case English) and none learning two. The Swiss "general secondary school," though unstreamed, would also be a fair counterpart.

The English equivalent of Hawick High School would probably be a large multi-lateral or comprehensive school:[1] the French (and possibly closer) equivalent would be a *lycée* with classical and modern sides—but the French "modern" side would correspond to the technical side at Hawick and its pupils would learn a foreign language, most probably English, while the "rural" and "modified" pupils would at present remain in the extension classes of the primary school, though the French Ministry of Education hope shortly to make more distinctive "secondary" arrangements for such pupils.

There also exist a few schools more closely corresponding to the English "comprehensive schools" — that is with setting in many subjects and no clearcut line dividing "academic" from "technical," "non-academic" and "modified" sides . Kirkcaldy High School is perhaps the best-known example.[2] Nothing exactly similar has yet materialised on the Continent but the Swedish "Unity schools" when fully developed, will be of similar type.

Purely non-academic secondary *departments* are fairly common, especially in large villages. Potential academic pupils from the primary department of the same school are transferred at 12 to the nearest available senior secondary school. Thus non-academic pupils at Denholm (Roxburghshire) remain where they are, while academic pupils go to Hawick.

Purely non-academic secondary *schools* only exist, generally in towns large enough to support a purely academic school nearby —towns that is, with a population of 50,000 or more. Sometimes however, one may find a non-academic Catholic secondary school in a rather smaller town where academic Catholic pupils attend the one senior secondary school, with a majority of non-Catholics.

---

[1] Multi-lateral schools have quite distinct " grammar ", " technical " and modern sides. Comprehensive schools may have as many as fifteen " streams " gradually fading off into one another, and it is difficult to say at which point the " grammar " element disappears.

[2] In fact Kirkcaldy High School is purely ' academic ", but since its intake is 25 per cent of the " twelve-plus " age group in the area which it serves, it has many pupils who would have been placed in the " A " Stream of an English Secondary Modern School. St. Andrew's School nearby, however, is a comprehensive school for Catholics in the Kirkcaldy area, and the one selective Catholic school for " academic " pupils in Fife as a whole. It is also open to Catholics in Fife to attend the ordinary public schools, and many do so, especially in the East Neuk (St. Andrews, Tayport, Cupar, etc.).

The reason is that, in such towns, Catholics nearly all belong to the working class and would not between them produce enough pupils able to follow an academic course *and* willing to stay on at school beyond the minimum leaving age—or if the pupils are willing, their parents may still want them to start earning as soon as possible. A similar and possibly larger problem exists in many English towns.

Purely academic public secondary schools are rarer in Scotland than almost anywhere in Europe. For this there are three reasons:

(a) Many academic pupils attend schools which also include a majority or a substantial minority of non-academic pupils (e.g. Hawick High School).

(b) The few wholly academic schools tend to be very large and are therefore thinner on the ground. They are mainly found in towns with a population of 50,000 and above, or serving a group of smaller towns. In England and on the Continent most towns with a population of 10,000 or above have at least one such school.

(c) In the cities a large proportion and sometimes a majority of middle-class pupils attend fee-paying schools, either grant-aided or (less frequently) independent.

The only country where they are rarer is the Republic of Ireland where they do not exist and where grant-aided schools are left virtually in possession of the field. But Ireland is a highly anomalous country with an archaic system which most thinking Irishmen dislike while unable to agree on how to replace it.[1] The main distinctive feature of Irish education is that primary schools are managed by priests and other clergy who deal directly with the Ministry of Education and must observe the Irish equivalent of the Schools (Scotland) Code, while secondary schools are all grant-aided or independent. There are definite resemblances to the pre-1872 Scottish set-up and still more perhaps to the arrangements prevailing in England before 1870. Furthermore a great deal of time is wasted on the compulsory study of what appears to be a dying language—there is hardly (if any) more Irish spoken in Ireland than there is Gaelic spoken in Scotland—of the two, Irish may even be losing ground a little faster.

In its organisation, as in its spirit and choice of curriculum described in the next two chapters, our educational system is not so close to England's as to Norway's or Sweden's—bearing in mind

---

[1] See my earlier book " Schools of Europe ".

however that everything starts and ends earlier, and that the third stage, that of definite preparation for University entrance through our equivalent of the Student-Examen, is somewhat compressed and not quite so thorough. We are I think, very conservative about these matters, despite the efforts of the Inspectorate and of the Advisory Council to get things moving. Our reluctance to change is due partly to our reverence for sound learning and the well-trodden ways of our forebears, and very largely to our fear of becoming like the English and of being absorbed by them in due course.

I should not devour the substance of my last chapter at this early stage, but feel I must state here my strongly-held conviction that this is due to a deep-seated inferiority complex, among the worst results of our anomalous constitutional position. Integrated with England we should modernise under the influence of Curzon Street.[1] With greater independence, such as Hamburg, Massachussets or Zurich enjoy, we could pick and choose, taking the best of what is being done or projected in England, as in Russia or Sweden, and without fearing to lose our identity thereby.

---

[1] Ministry of Education, London.

47

CHAPTER III

Aims And Spirit Of The System

The aims of Scottish Education are officially stated in the Schools (Scotland) Code of 1949. It will be seen that they are not very different from those of English Education as set forth in the 1944 Education Act.

"... it shall be the duty of the local education authority for every area, so far as their powers extend, to contribute towards the spiritual, moral, mental and physical development of the community by securing that efficient education throughout these stages shall be available to meet the needs of the population of their area . . . and the schools available for an area shall not be deemed to be sufficient unless they are sufficient in number, character and equipment to afford for all pupils opportunities for education offering such variety of instruction and training as may be desirable in view of their different ages, abilities and aptitudes, and of the different periods for which they may be expected to remain at school, including practical instruction and training appropriate to their respective needs." (Education Act, Sections 7 and 8).

The Schools Code (Sections 18 and 19) goes into more detail and makes specific demands with which it has not everywhere been possible to comply. I have underlined those requirements which are at present the hardest to fulfil, because they presuppose a sufficient number of teachers of exceptional ability and/or an artistic turn of mind, decidedly smaller classes, and more suitable buildings in more attractive surroundings.

"Subject to the provisions of this Code it shall be the duty of the Education Authority to secure that the education given in any school is in accordance with the scheme prepared by the Education Authority under Section 7 and approved by the Secretary of State under Section 65 of the Act of 1946, is adequate and efficient, is suited to the age, ability and aptitude of the pupils and is in accordance with the scheme of work approved for the school under Regulation 20 of this Code. Special provision shall be made for the instruction of backward and retarded pupils *and for the development of the special gifts of pupils who show exceptional ability.*

" In the conduct of the school from day to day all reasonable care shall be taken to train the pupils in habits of personal hygiene and cleanliness, *of correct speech and of good manners;* to cultivate the qualities of truthfulness, honesty, self-control and consideration for man and beast; *to foster a love of beauty;* and to encourage industry, self-reliance, forethought and a sense of responsibility to the community."

In both countries, theory diverges from practice and in Scotland it probably diverges more than in England. At least 80% of the school day is taken up with the teaching of examinable subjects. These may have a character-building or personality-developing value, which depends essentially on the way in which they are taught and on the character and personality of individual teachers. But the purpose, both of the teachers and of such pupils as have one, is that *measurable* and *useful* proficiency shall be achieved. Non-examinable subjects generally come a poor third to examinable subjects of limited practical use, and these a poor second to " major subjects " which will serve as an important part of one's working qualifications later —essentially English, Mathematics, Science and one or more Modern Languages.

My impression is that in both countries the fine phrases of the Education Act and the Schools Code, and the spirit they embody, are regarded as something that has to be there and which one tries to put across in Assembly and on Speech Day, while the dispensing of a mainly academic education is treated as the real business of the school and its teachers.

Nevertheless English secondary education conforms more closely to the spirit of the two Acts than its Scottish counterpart has done hitherto. This is partly because the pressure of time is less—it starts a year earlier and, for the abler pupil, it usually ends a year later.

Another reason is the historical one that Public Schools, in the English sense, have served as a model for all schools in England to a far greater extent than they have in Scotland. They have been in the field much longer, and have educated a much larger slice of the middle class generally, and therefore of those who form public opinion and organise public education. In consequence the average Englishman expects even a day school to do many things not normally expected of schools in Scotland.

The main reason perhaps is that the aim of the full academic course in England, leading up to "A" Level and Open Scholarship examinations, is to prepare pupils for work *under university conditions* and teach them how to think. The aim of the same but rather shorter course in Scotland, leading up to "Highers" and the competitive bursary examinations, is to give them a " broad liberal education " and in practice to teach them as much as possible. A very general comment of those with whom I discussed this subject could be worded thus: " Scottish examinations test factual knowledge rather than ability to organise and use that knowledge, or reading ' round that subject '."

It seems to me that ability to think is, under modern conditions, when the sum total of human knowledge is in any case far beyond anybody's mental storage capacity, more valuable than ready command of a large battery of grammatical rules and assorted facts. The process by which this ability is developed is also, in itself, more valuable to the human personality as a whole than the process by which facts and rules, beyond the basic essentials, are drummed in.

So far as I can judge the real, if no longer the official aims of Scottish Education are to ensure basic literacy, numeracy and godliness for all, and to get the "lad o' pairts" (and now the " lass o' pairts " also) to and through University. These are admirable objects so far as they go, though secondary teachers pay less attention than they should to developing the qualities which will get their pupils *through* University.

The system, though it probably gives more generous opportunities to the good-average pupil, and extends him more fully than most others, is defective in two main respects: —

(a) because of the inadequate liaison between Senior Secondary Schools and Universities, it does less than its best for the really bright. This did not matter so much when universities were prepared to do what many secondary schools, especially the smaller ones, had left undone;

(b) it has not adapted itself to the fact that average pupils now remain at school for two or three years after they have acquired the basic skills as far as they are likely to need them, or at least think themselves likely to need them.

Both these weaknesses are common to nearly all European countries, and in some of them far graver than here. The extreme case, as regards inadequate preparation for university work, is probably Belgium where 80% of students fail their first-year exams on first attempt and 60% to 65% never get any further even after a second try and possibly a third or fourth.[1]

One criticism often made is that Scottish Education is too heavily biased on the Arts side, while today more scientists and technicians are needed. This, so far as it is true, applies throughout Western Europe with the possible exception of England and some of the German *Länder*. But I am not sure how far this criticism is justified.

English is an Arts subject, but in an English-speaking country it is essential to all scientific study; French, German and Russian also have their uses to the practical scientist. Some knowledge of Geography is indispensable in a world whose industry and commerce are more international than ever before. Even the less demonstrably "useful" subjects, for instance History, are more valuable than the layman might think. Our entry into the Common Market will bring us into closer contact with many people whom we shall now have to try and understand: we can learn at least as much about them by studying their history *intelligently taught* than in any other way.

Nor is it certain that we shall always need as many scientists and technicians as we need at the present time. This depends on the future evolution of our society. If all goes well, knowledge of how to use our leisure may be as important as having a good working qualification, largely acquired after leaving school, owing to its very specialised nature. If things go less well, a handful of survivors may have to reconstruct the world from poisoned ruins, and in that case the virtues formed and the abilities developed by a Christian and classical education may be a far greater asset than knowledge of processes which have perished with the material equipment they required and with the highly developed economy which they served.

A more serious criticism is that Scottish Education does not

---

[1] In Scotland the first-year failure rate is in the region of 30 per cent for those who have only completed five years in a Senior Secondary School—the minimum qualification for attempting "Highers". It is about 15 per cent for those who have completed six years.

prepare our children for life *in this country*.[1] If they follow an academic curriculum a large proportion of them will be surplus to Scottish requirements and will therefore have to leave —which they may do even without economic compulsion, because the opportunities furth of Scotland are not only more numerous but on the whole more attractive than those existing here.

If they follow a non-academic curriculum they will in most cases be fit only for unskilled labour, until such time as this side of education, both in school and thereafter, is taken far more seriously and organised far more effectively than at present. Again they will have to emigrate, because the shortage of skilled labour is one of several causes which discourage those with capital, even in this country, from investing it in the development of Scottish industry. The other and more important causes of recurrent unemployment have little if anything to do with education: they include our more remote position (vis-a-vis Southern and Central England, though not vis-a-vis Northern Europe) and the necessity for English politicians of keeping as much as possible of London and the Midlands on their side, by maintaining a fairly high standard of living there.

The solution to the first problem is mainly political. Greater decentralisation would provide more opportunities for Scotsmen to run things in Scotland: a complete break might provide more opportunities still and, in the context of the Common Market, would not disrupt our economy to the same extent as hitherto.

The second problem again requires a largely political solution. Somebody must have power to attract industry to Scotland by means not open to the present administration at St. Andrew's House, responsible as it is to a mainly English Parliament. At the same time there must be far greater insistence upon effective practical education, both in the secondary schools and thereafter.

The academic bias so often criticized in our system is fully justifiable while we remain a subordinate, outlying and somewhat depressed part of the United Kingdom as at present organised. If our children have to emigrate, it is far better for

---

[1] This criticism no longer applies with equal force everywhere, and some authorities at least have made a determined and successful effort to bring academic and non-academic curricula up to date.

But it is still very generally believed to be true, and this is nearly as damning as if it actually were true in all or most respects. The effectiveness of any type of education depends very largely on the confidence which it inspires.

them to emigrate as members of the middle class than as unskilled labourers.

An interesting point made by one of my Jedburgh colleagues was that English schools tend to produce (a) *leaders* (in the Public Schools, the Direct Grant Schools and to some extent the Sixth Forms of Maintained Grammar Schools) and (b) *led*, while the Scottish system aims at producing, and regards as its ideal product, responsible independent individuals who are at their best in non-hierarchical occupations — for instance doctors, engineers and lawyers. How far is that true?

I think there is quite a lot in it. Character formation and training in leadership have never been major aims of the typically Scottish school, though they have happened as an incidental part of the educational process: on the other hand it has been customary for all to attend, though not always completing their course, schools from which one *could* and ideally *did* proceed to the Universities.

But this has not necessarily been planned as educational policy: it is rather due to the national religion and temperament and to geographical factors. The Scottish National Church is definitely Protestant and non-hierarchical, and has taken the nation with it, to the extent that *Scottish* Catholics and Episcopalians show many of the same characteristics as their Presbyterian fellow-citizens. The English National Church is hierarchical and very marginally Protestant; and the English naturally sort themselves out into the best and the rest.

While County and City Councils tend to be politically dominated, as in England, by Socialists sitting as such or by Conservatives in the guise of Independents, Rate-Payers, Moderates, Progressives, etc., the political influence in education is perhaps less evident. One does not generally find schools organised to serve political ends in the same way as the Leicestershire Experiment and the London comprehensive schools have been planned—or appear to have been planned—in order to mix the social classes and the ability groups and promote a feeling of equality. Nor does one find the veiled purpose of keeping " the lower orders " in their proper " station " which still seems to linger in parts of Southern England. The Scottish Education Department keeps a tighter rein on over-experimental authorities and prods the indolent ones more vigorously than does its English counterpart: it is better placed to do so, since it has fewer authorities, schools and pupils to watch.

Where politics and religion sometimes come in is in the making of appointments and especially of senior appointments, while one may observe a certain difference not of purpose but of emphasis, as between the authorities of cities and mainly industrial counties, and those of mainly rural counties with a more scattered population and smaller towns. The difference is that the former spend more on educational welfare and on what the French call " *les activités para-scolaires* " (school and youth camps, organised trips abroad, etc.) while the latter concentrate heavily on education in its traditional sense. This has no political implications. There is greater need for these marginal activities in cities and in counties such as Fife and Renfrew, where the home and local community background may, on balance, be less " educative ". In Roxburgh or Inverness, for instance, there are greater possibilities for healthy outdoor recreation on the spot— local life may be more active and more varied—while " education proper " costs rather more per child, since many small schools have to be maintained and staffed, and a good deal of transport has to be provided.

As between Catholic and other public schools, the main difference is that the latter treat religion as part of the curriculum —one subject among eight or ten which every pupil must generally take, while the former do not "departmentalise" it in this way: they make it permeate the whole atmosphere and aim to have every subject taught by a practising Catholic wherever this is compatible with reasonable academic efficiency. Children are sent to " ordinary " schools to be educated. The religious instruction will in fact be Protestant, but the *raison d'être* of the school is simply to educate, not to educate in a Protestant way. A Catholic school, however, exists in order to give a Catholic education and children are sent there in order to receive it— unless, as sometimes happens in the Western Highlands and the Isles, they are Protestants who have no other school to attend, and for whom the usual contracting-out arrangements are made.

In such cases they are entitled to absent themselves from morning assembly, or come in after prayers to hear any notices that may be given out. They may also absent themselves from religious instruction. Catholics in non-Catholic schools normally do likewise. According to Dom Mark Dilworth, O.S.B., who has unrivalled knowledge of the Western Highlands, many Protestant children, in such circumstances, still take part in all

54

the religious activities of the school, whereas Catholic pupils in Protestant schools almost invariably contract out.

It is, of course, impossible to contract out of the Catholic atmosphere of a Catholic school. Since it is in this, rather than in specific observances or instruction, that its special character lies, Protestant parents may see little point in compelling their children to be "different". Protestant schools have a less distinctive atmosphere, and by contracting out of prayers and religious instruction Catholic pupils miss all that is specifically Protestant about them. Furthermore their priests generally insist that they do so.

There is some dissatisfaction among practising Protestants with the way in which religion is taught in most public schools. It seems that the terms according to which their schools were transferred to Local Authorities (religious instruction to continue "according to use and wont") have not been fully honoured and that the hours of religious instruction on the time-table have been considerably reduced—from one a day when the schools were taken over, to the present one or two a week.

Lack of suitably qualified and wholeheartedly Christian teachers is not always a sufficient excuse, since there are quite large areas (e.g. Northern Hebrides, Isle of Skye) where the great majority of teachers would be well able to cope.

In this connection the comments made by Mr. W. Scott Dickson, of Kirkcaldy, in a letter published by the *Glasgow Herald* (3rd October, 1961) seem very relevant.

(1) "Under the present Regulations there is no provision for the recognition of a qualification in religious education. It is true that Chap. IV and V teachers get some training in the subject, and that one may even earn a diploma or a higher diploma in the subject but all this training has no professional importance simply because it cannot be recognised under the Regulations.

(2) A probationer teacher whether Chap. IV or Chap. V who is employed full time in religious education cannot even earn his final certificate unless he is prepared to teach some other subject in which he can be inspected.

(3) This situation arises from the fact that religious education by Act of Parliament is outwith the scope of the Secretary of State for Scotland and therefore outwith the scope of the Scottish Education Department.

(4) There is no salary scale for specialists in religious

education. There cannot be since they are not teachers! Those
who are employed are either paid on the basis of their
" recognised " professional qualifications or on some *ad hoc* basis
negotiated between the local education authority and the Secretary of State who must consult with the National Joint Council
before making a decision.

(5) Any young man therefore who wishes to become a
specialist in religious education has to face the fact that unless
he has a double qualification, one professional to secure his
salary and one non-professional so that he may know what to
" teach " and how to " teach " it, he will get nowhere. There is
no parallel that I know of to this demand.

(6) Moreover any young man who, out of the conviction
that religious education is the foundation of all character
building and therefore *the* subject in the curriculum, trains in
that subject will find that even if he has the additional
professional qualification to ensure placing on a scale he has
no chance of promotion. There is no Department of Religious
Education. He cannot become either a specialist assistant or
a head of a department and in consequence he cannot become a
depute head teacher or a head teacher. There is no promotion
available to him at all.

It follows that although it is said to be the most important
subject in our schools and must on no account be discontinued
without a plebiscite, religious education is professionally a dead
end and it is not to be wondered at that young men with ability
and brains opt for teaching subjects with prospects.

The steps which require to be taken to correct the situation
are few. In the first place, the training regulations should be
altered to allow recognition of religious education as a special
subject in the secondary schools as mathematics and science, etc.,
are recognised. This would enable the specialist in religious
education to obtain a Chap. V qualification. In the second
place, while an academic course acceptable to the powers that be
as of Honours grade is planned and then made available,
recognition should be given as a temporary measure to those
who have obtained a B.D. with distinction or some equivalent
qualification from a theological faculty or college. In the third
place, a Department of Religious Education should be instituted
in at least each of the senior secondary schools, thus opening
the way to the appointment of specialist assistants and heads.
Lastly, the headship of such a department should be accepted as

qualifying its holder to apply for a post as a head teacher or depute head teacher.

It is recognised that it may be argued that this will involve a change in the Education Act. If that is true then let the Act be changed. It is surely better that the Act be changed than that we continue to talk about doing something which no one has authority to see is done."

The main differences between public and fee-paying schools are considered in Chapter IV. As regards *purpose* the obvious difference is that fee-paying schools are not obliged to educate *everybody* nor, for that matter, everybody who is prepared to pay the fees. They only accept those pupils who seem intellectually able to complete the full academic course and reasonably likely to do so. The idea of pulling out at the minimum age and taking a job simply does not occur to their pupils and would not be countenanced by parents or masters concerned with those pupils. Because they have no early leaving problem, and for other reasons to be discussed later, they are much better schools *for those who attend them*. Whether their existence also benefits the community at large is another matter, extremely difficult to argue about convincingly, since one has first to prove the validity of one's original standpoint, namely that the nation must have a properly educated *élite,* or conversely that the milk needs to retain the cream, and the " proofs " advanced by either side themselves tend to be rather subjective and only to persuade those who are already on that side emotionally, but cannot think up good reasons to justify themselves.

Within the fee-paying " system " the main difference of purpose between Grant-Aided (Direct Grant) schools and English-type " Public Schools " is that the former set out to do the same job as public secondary schools, but to do it more efficiently thanks to their selective entry and more favourable staffing ratio, while the latter set out to do the same job as similar schools in England. Furthermore the Grant-Aided schools normally prepare their pupils for Scottish examinations—with few exceptions the " Public Schools " prepare theirs for G.C.E. and for Oxford and Cambridge open scholarships.[1]

---

[1] Fort Augustus prepares its boys for Scottish examinations, partly because 85 per cent of them are Scots, partly because it is a relatively small school, for which the broadly-based Scottish curriculum is more suitable. A number of the Scottish Grant-Aided Schools are at the same time " Public Schools " by virtue of their membership in the Head Masters' Conference. They also take the Scottish examinations. See Chapter V.

Not unnaturally the Grant-Aided schools get a much larger proportion of their senior pupils through "Highers" than the public secondary schools. It is impossible to compare the academic results of Grant-Aided and "Public School" candidates since the examinations they attempt are not equivalent. As between public secondary schools in different areas comparison, though possible, would be extremely misleading and would give no indication of the relative merits of Labour and Conservative education authorities, or of their administrative and teaching staff.

For instance 17.8% of school leavers completed the Senior Secondary course in Edinburgh (1959-60) as against 9.2% in Renfrew, 4.8% in Midlothian and 24.1% in Sutherland. But this has more to do with the type of population and the opportunities available for 15-year-old leavers than with the policy of the authorities concerned. The proportion of "minimum-age" leavers for these areas was 56.8% for Edinburgh (it is always fairly low in capital cities), 74.9% for Renfrew, 83.2% for Midlothian and 44.1% for Sutherland.

To compare the performance of pupils at Catholic and other public secondary schools would be even more difficult. One must first remember that the average run of Catholics come from less cultured homes than the average run of Protestants, except in those areas where the Old Religion is very strongly entrenched, and there the secondary schools normally take pupils of both persuasions, often making "simultaneous" arrangements for religious instruction as in Germany and Switzerland. The secondary school in Castlebay, (Isle of Barra) for instance, is not a Catholic school in the same sense as Holy Cross Academy in Edinburgh: it is a public school with a 95% majority of Catholic pupils.

Secondly, and in consequence of this social "weighting" of the Catholic population as a whole, it often happens that non-academic Catholic pupils will go to a junior secondary school of their own faith, while academic ones go to an "ordinary" senior secondary school and contract out of religious instruction. We are therefore left with a very small number of Catholic senior secondary schools, often with an underweight "certificate" side (because of the social composition of the Catholic body) and a much larger number of "ordinary" senior secondary schools, usually with a rather larger certificate side and sometimes with no non-academic pupils.

One last point. Many of the criticisms levelled against Scottish Education, as regards its aims and spirit, boil down to saying that it is not English, and that, as on the Continent, it is too limited in its objectives and too formal in its outlook. These criticisms are only valid if one accepts that what is English is necessarily right in itself, or at any rate right for Scotland as well as for England.

Scottish schools undoubtedly set themselves a more limited task, and this was always so. Parents, the local community and the rugged countryside itself have traditionally done the rest. So it is in Scandinavia and in Switzerland. In the context of the small burgh, with moors and forests all around and loch or sea nearby, this division of labour is sensible enough and continues to yield first-class results. It ensures that the school's time is taken up with doing what only the school can do, and that no conflict of ethics or loyalties can arise between it and the home.

The atmosphere of crowded cities and faceless housing estates is in a sense less typically Scottish, but three-fifths at least of all Scotsmen live in it—and here perhaps the existing combination of strictly " functional " school and often indifferent home is not fully adequate. Whether the education gap should be bridged by changing the character of the schools and sacrificing solid academic work to more esoteric ideals and pursuits, or in some other way, is a question which I propose to consider in another place.

CHAPTER IV

Contents and Methods of Education

Scottish children normally spend seven years at a primary school, starting at the age of five. This compares with six years from the age of five in England, seven years from the age of seven in Norway, four, six or seven years from the age of seven in Sweden and four, six or eight years from the age of six in Germany, Switzerland and several other Continental countries, where less able pupils complete their formal education in the primary schools. Fuller details are given in my book, *Schools of Europe*, and in pamphlets issued by most Ministries of Education.

The great majority of Scottish adolescents spend three years in a junior secondary school or in the non-academic streams of a senior secondary or omnibus school. This compares with four years at secondary modern and comprehensive schools in England, a year in the continuation school or three years at the *realskola* in Norway, and three to five years at the general secondary school in Switzerland, depending on the age of entry.

The standard course for *academic pupils* lasts five years in senior secondary schools or the academic stream of an omnibus school. A high but variable proportion of those who enter senior secondary schools fail to complete the course (see the Working Party's report on *Early Leaving*,[1] and the annual

---

[1] This Working Party was appointed by the Secretary of State, after a pilot survey had been carried out by a committee of the Scottish Headmasters' Association. It found that many pupils, attempting the stiff " Highers " course, got out of their depth, allowed themselves to be discouraged and therefore left without *any* certificate. It therefore recommended that the old Lower Grade should be replaced by a new and slightly less ambitious Ordinary Grade, corresponding to " O " Level in England. This would serve as a reinsurance for candidates who were not reasonably certain to pass on the Higher Grade in any particular subject and as an objective for those who were definitely unlikely to do so. Strong candidates could still by-pass " O " Grade in particular subjects, and would be encouraged to do so. The new Ordinary Grade

reports " Education in Scotland" issued by the Scottish Education Department). In the academic year 1959-60, out of 24,888 pupils leaving from supposedly five-year courses, 4763 had not even completed the third-year programme: 12,523 altogether (more than half) had not completed the fourth year programme, and therefore *could not* have taken *any* certificate. 3304 had completed the fourth year programme and *could* therefore have taken " Lower Leavings" but not "Highers". Very few in fact, had taken a certificate. 4209 had completed the course and a further 4452 had gone beyond it to do a sixth year and exceptionally a seventh—in the case of pupils entering the course a year early by special permission of the Education Authority concerned.

The proportion of about 35% completing or over-running the course is substantially the same as in Germany and Sweden. It is a little lower than in England where the course is more difficult to enter, and where academic pupils do not normally attend the same schools as non-academic ones, and therefore tend to lose contact with them. But the proportion of those achieving an intermediate objective — in our case "Lower Leavings", now to be replaced by "Ordinary Grade", is much lower than in England, Germany or Scandinavia, and the proportion of those leaving without any qualification is decidedly higher. The reasons are explained in the *Report on Early Leaving*: the main one is that the intermediate objective was pitched far too high. Another reason is that in most countries the "Ordinary Grade" equivalent is taken two or three years before the "Highers" equivalent, and is taken by all (in England) or by all those who do not seem reasonably likely to take " Highers". In some countries (e.g. West Germany) the mere fact of having got into the last two classes of the senior secondary school automatically confers the "Ordinary" qualification even though one has by-passed the examination itself. This is *not*

---

is being taken for the first time in May 1962. The Lower Grade was last taken in March 1961.

The timing of this examination has been changed because "Lower Leavings" were normally taken, in their weaker subjects, by fifth-year candidates, and as a fourth-year examination only by fourth-year leavers, and in one subject alone. The new examination will be taken in the fourth year in a range of subjects some of which may only have been started in the second or third year. It has therefore been felt desirable to allow another two months of preparation. To simplify administrative arrangements, the Higher Grade will now also be taken in May, and presumably the Advanced Grade likewise, when it comes into existence.

the case in Scotland and also explains the high proportion of pupils leaving *without any certificate.* 51% of pupils as we have seen, could not have taken a certificate, but of the 49% who, chronologically speaking, could have done so, a substantial number, including nearly all the fourth-year leavers, did not. This unsatisfactory situation should right itself with the appearance of the new " Ordinary" Grade.

The primary *curriculum* is, in its essentials, the same as in most European countries because the same basic skills are required, and as everywhere each class is taken by one teacher in all or nearly all subjects.

For purposes of comparison, here are specimen weekly programmes for a class of ten-year-olds in Scotland, England, Norway, Iceland and France respectively. This is a sixth class in Scotland and in England, a fifth class in France and a fourth in Norway and Iceland.

ENGLAND
PRIMARY SCHOOL TIME-TABLES

1. Rural C. of E. Primary School (at Eastry, Kent).

	HOURS		HOURS
Diaries & Spelling. ("Diaries" include composition, and individual and class criticism thereof) - - -	$2\frac{1}{2}$	Things Began," History including "follow-up" by class teacher & pupils. -	$3\frac{1}{2}$
Spelling Test (APPROX) -	$\frac{1}{2}$	Singing, Hymn Singing & Choir Practice - - -	$1\frac{1}{4}$
Group Reading (APPROX) -	$\frac{3}{4}$	Church of England Teaching and Religious Instruc-	
Optional English* (APPROX) - - - -	$3\frac{1}{4}$	tion (Scripture) - -	$1\frac{1}{4}$
Maths - - - - -	$3\frac{1}{4}$	Geography - - - -	$1\frac{1}{4}$
Mental Arithmetic (APPROX) - - - -	$\frac{1}{4}$	Physical Education - -	$1\frac{1}{2}$
Art and/or Craft (APPROX) - - - -	$2\frac{1}{2}$	Games & Extra-Mural Activities: Boys - - -	2
B.B.C. (Broadcast Service, Junior Science, "How		Girls - - -	$\frac{3}{4}$
		Needlework Girls - - -	$1\frac{1}{4}$

* Optional English includes vocabulary work, drama, poetry and "books" compiled by the pupils on Canterbury Cathedral, local brickfields, etc. The option rests with the Class Teacher, who in this instance is also the Head Master. The pupils are *not* given the option of playing about instead of working.

2. County Suburban Primary School (at South Wigston, Leicestershire).

(a) one class, with ability range of I.Q 80-120, and, mainly working in small groups.

	HOURS		HOURS
Maths (includes "Algebraic Experience Material" for some groups)	4-50	TV "Discovering Science"	35
		Choral Speech and Movement/Art & Craft	2
English, Reading and Literature	1-35	Movement (including Drama)	1
"Topic"	1-10	"Adventure in Music"	30
Language	35	Singing	35
Discussion	35	Class Time Table (see below)	4
Poetry & Prose Composition	1-10	Physical Education	1-5
		Games	1

"Class Time Table" includes Geography, Science, History and Religious Education, not necessarily planned on a weekly basis. An hour of this time is given each fortnight to a Public Library visit.

Some Maths and English periods may be combined in double-length periods whose programme includes elements of both subjects, e.g. a talk about the Aswan Dam, with some discussion of the mathematics involved.

(b) Another class, similarly organised.

	HOURS		HOURS
Maths (including some Algebra & Geometry for brighter groups)	4-50	Class Time Table (see above)	4
		English or Orchestra	1
I.T.V. Maths	30	Singing	1-5
English "Topic"	1-45	Art & Craft Room (some groups on Movement & Orchestra)	2
Written Work	2-20	Physical Education	1
Reading	1-10	Games	1

SCOTLAND
PRIMARY SCHOOL TIME-TABLES

	HOURS		HOURS
Arithmetic - - - -	4	Nature Study; Science - - -	1
English including Reading and Interpretation, Speech Training, Formal Grammar, Oral & Written Language, Expression Exercises, Spelling and Dictation - - - -	$8\frac{1}{4}$	Boys' Handwork; Girls' Sewing - - - -	$2\frac{3}{4}$
		Art - - - - -	1
		Music - - - - -	1
		Physical Education - -	$2\frac{1}{2}$
		Religious Education - -	$2\frac{1}{2}$
History - - - - -	1	
Geography - - - -	1	The above time-table was supplied by the Headmistress
Handwriting - - - -	$\frac{1}{2}$	of Toryglen School, Glasgow.

SCOTLAND*

	PERIODS		PERIODS
Arithmetic (incl. Mental Arith.) - -	8	Nature Study (incl. $\frac{1}{2}$ period Schools Broadcast) - - - -	$1\frac{1}{2}$
Spelling - - - - -	5	Physical Education - -	1
Composition - - -	2	Needlework or Handwork - - -	2
Recitation, poems, etc. -	2	
Reading - - - - -	$5\frac{1}{2}$	Music - - - - -	1
English Grammar - -	$2\frac{1}{2}$	
Writing - - - - -	$1\frac{1}{2}$	Art - - - - -	2
Stories and History (incl. 1 period Schools Broadcast) - - - -	3	Religious Instruction -	1
		Sports (boys) or Library (girls) - -	2
Geography (incl. $\frac{1}{2}$ period Schools Broadcast) - - - -	$2\frac{1}{2}$	Projects, etc. - - -	$2\frac{1}{2}$
		Averaging 35 minutes each	

* The time-table in Scotland, as in England, is less strictly regulated than in most Continental countries. The above is a representative specimen, obtained at Newtown St. Boswells (Roxburghshire). Depending on the headmaster's views as to the relative importance of certain subjects, and the staffing situation in any particular school, there may for instance be more music, more grammar, less art, fewer broadcasts, etc.

THE QUADRANGLE & STATUE OF THE FOUNDER,
GEORGE HERIOT'S COLLEGE, EDINBURGH.

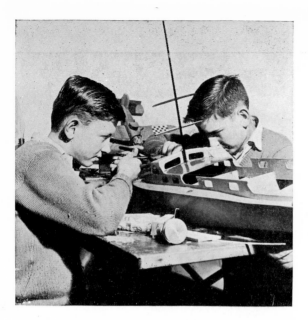

MODEL MAKING AT RANNOCH SCHOOL

WORK AT THE SLUICE GATE FOR THE
HYDRO ELECTRIC TURBINE
AT RANNOCH SCHOOL

NORWAY

	PERIODS PER WEEK
Religion	2
Norwegian	6
History	1
Geography	2
Natural Science	2
Arithmetic	5
Writing	2
Drawing	2
Singing	2
Handicrafts	3
Physical Training	3
	TOTAL 30

Norwegian schools normally work six days a week, mornings only. Periods last 45 minutes.

ICELAND

	PERIODS
Icelandic (reading composition, etc.)	7
Writing (copy)	3
Arithmetic	4
Religious Instruction	2
History, Geology, Nature Study	5
Handicrafts	2
Singing	1
Drawing	2
Sports	2-3
At teacher's disposal (free activity)	1

Total 29-30 periods of 40 mins.

FRANCE

	HOURS
Moral Instruction	1
French (incl. reading)	9
History and Geography	$1\frac{1}{2}$
Arithmetic	5
Nature Study	$1\frac{1}{2}$
Drawing or Handicrafts	1
Singing	1
Supervised preparation	5

	HOURS
Physical Education, Sports, organised walks, etc	$2\frac{1}{2}$
Morning and afternoon breaks	$2\frac{1}{2}$
	TOTAL 30

French Primary Schools, normally work five days a week, including Saturdays but excluding Thursdays.

It will be seen that English Primary School time-tables are highly flexible, due to the exceptional freedom allowed to Headmasters and Class Teachers in England. It would in fact have been impossible to find a "typical" time-table, except by averaging out a large number of individual specimens. Eastry School has relatively limited facilities, hence (I imagine) the heavy reliance on the B.B.C. South Wigston School is probably more "progressive" than most, as the "eleven-plus" examination has been scrapped by Leicestershire. A more conventional and examination-bent school with streamed classes might be expected to have time-tables similar to those of Toryglen School and Newtown St. Boswells School.

On the Continent and in Scandinavia the Ministry of Education or the corresponding sub-national authority usually specifies what subjects are to be taught and what time allowance each subject shall have—in some cases it may even state at what time a particular subject or division of a subject shall be taught, so that at 10 a.m. on a Monday morning, for instance, every pupil in the country is about to start on a dictation. Scottish Primary School Heads have greater freedom than their Continental Colleagues, in that their time-table is not imposed, nor is there a rigid time allowance for each subject; but they have less freedom than English Heads, in that their schemes of work, embodying a time allowance if not an actual time-table, must be approved by the Director of Education and by Her Majesty's Inspectors. The position in Holland is approximately the same as in Scotland, but there the "approving authority" is the Ministry of Education, while the curriculum and sometimes the time-table are drawn up not by the Headmaster but by the governing body of the school. This will be a parents' association in the case of Catholic or Protestant schools, and the Provost and Bailies (Mayor and Aldermen) in the case of public schools.

Teaching methods in our primary schools are probably a little more conservative than in England: the use of corporal punishment and the setting of homework are certainly more frequent. We also have many more small schools, with one or two teachers only.

Primary school teachers in Norway and Iceland set considerably more homework than here, either because their schools only meet in the mornings, or because exceptional arrangements prevail—e.g. alternate-day or alternate-week schooling in remote areas with a scattered population.

In their report on Primary Education the Advisory Council recommended the abolition of compulsory homework in primary schools, as being contrary to the spirit in which they felt that primary education should be carried on. They felt however that there was a strong case for *voluntary* homework set in accordance with a child's individual interests and hinted at a possible lengthening of the school day in order to allow what is now set as homework to be worked into the time-table.

On the whole I am with them, with two important reservations.

(1) I think there is a case for *some* homework in P.V, P.VI, and P.VII—not exceeding thirty or forty minutes a day altogether—and at the same time for *less* homework in S.I and S.II. the sudden change from *no* homework to $1\frac{1}{2}$-2 hours a night would have, I feel, a very unsettling effect.[1]

(2) I do not believe the work of the very small school, in which three, four, or seven classes are taken in one room by the same teacher, can be carried on without the setting of some homework from P.IV onwards, unless the school is so designed that it contains a room where pupils in some of these classes can work quietly at their appointed task while the teacher takes the rest in another room.

The same Report makes many criticisms of the existing curriculum and methods, on which I do not feel qualified to comment, except to say that every teacher, both primary and secondary, should read them and consider how far they are applicable in his or her case.

In the main I think they are more or less applicable throughout Europe, because everywhere curricula and methods are devised by people who have forgotten what it was like being a child, and who have never known what it is to be non-academic.

I would however add a few miscellaneous points of my own.

(1) Since a number of single-school teachers[2] happen to be *men* and have to take *infants*, it would be desirable to provide courses for *infant masters*. Normally infants should be taken by a woman: on the other hand it is a good thing that older primary pupils should be taken by a man, and it is often more convenient for a small community, especially in a remote area, to have a man as its teacher, because he can take a number of other duties—sessions clerk, registrar, chairman of various local bodies.

---

1 This argument was challenged as irrelevant by one of my London critics. I believe, however, that Scottish pupils, on arrival at their secondary schools, get into their stride much faster than English pupils. This may be due to their more thorough grounding and their greater age (12 plus instead of 11 plus) but the fact that they have already been faced with homework may also help. Here would be a promising field for research.

2 There exists no special name for teachers in charge of a single-teacher school. I have therefore taken the liberty of inventing one, viz. " single-school teacher ".

(2) In localities with a single-teacher school it might sometimes be desirable to make compulsory schooling start at the age of six, especially where the teacher happens to be a man. Mothers in such places are not normally working, and the many European countries where schooling starts at the age of six or seven do not necessarily fall behind us educationally. Norway, Sweden and Holland are level with us, Switzerland may be slightly ahead, so far as I can judge from visits to their schools and fairly frequent contact with their people. Here again, research into the advantages and disadvantages of our earlier start might be worthwhile.

(3) I found a considerable lack of agreement as to how certain basic processes should be taught.

For instance children may be taught to read pages, sentences, words or letters in the first instance, and in various ways which I do not feel qualified to describe I started by learning the alphabet as such (orally), then was taught to build words of increasing size with the letters as I learnt to recognise them. Since I could read the daily papers in my native language (French) at the age of six, I presume this method was fairly sound, but nearly all modern authorities are against it.[1]

Subtraction may be taught in a number of ways. *Decomposition* is the traditional one but has been largely ousted by *equal addition*. For the benefit of non-teachers and those who live in a purely secondary world I have tried to explain these methods below.

Question Subtract 29 from 67.
(a) by decomposition.
       9 from 7 won't go: "borrow" one from 60.
       9 from 17 leaves 8: 2 from 5 leaves 3.
       Answer: 38.

---

[1] The alphabetic method is still widely used by Icelandic parents, many of whom educate their children at home until they are nine or ten and can be sent to the small boarding schools of very sparsely populated areas. It is also used in Icelandic rural schools where the nearest children enrol at seven while others, living further away, only enrol at eight and are taught at home meantime.

It is thought to be slower than more "modern" methods and is therefore not normally used in town schools, but the results may be more lasting, and the general level of popular education in Iceland is probably the highest in the world. This however may be due to national tradition, climate and lack of distractions rather than to the educational methods used, and it was already so when the alphabetic method was employed throughout Europe.

(b) by equal addition.

9 from 7 won't go: add one before the 7, and compensate by changing the 20 into a 30.

9 from 17 leaves 8: 3 from 6 leaves 3.

Answer: 38.

Long Division again may be taught in a number of ways. It occurs towards the end of the primary course, but I am told that intending teachers are *not* taught how to put it across.

(4) A very good point applicable to secondary schools also, was made by one of my better-known " contacts ". It is that " Art " should not consist simply of drawing, painting and plasticine modelling but should include the whole aesthetic side of life: how to lay a table attractively, how to arrange the furniture and flowers in a room, how to choose curtains of a colour pleasing in itself and matching whatever else is already there. I do not think one can make an " art appreciator " in the conventional sense, of every pupil—but they should all be helped to develop a sense of beauty, order and design.

The transfer or " promotion " procedure at the end of the primary school course is substantially the same as over most of England, but local authorities have slightly less discretion in making their own arrangements since their promotion schemes must be submitted to and approved by the Scottish Education Department. The other main differences are that transfer takes place, on an average, a year later—viz. at 12 plus rather than 11 plus, and that a much higher proportion of pupils are originally placed in an " academic " school (i.e. a " pure " senior secondary school only found in cities and large towns) or the " academic " stream of a school also taking " non-academic " pupils.[1]

The procedure involves Moray House Intelligence Tests, taken in P.VI and P.VII and averaged out: Moray House attainment tests in English and Arithmetic: and consideration of the class teacher's report. In England the transfer procedure involves only one I.Q. test, but a variety of tests are used: all have 100 as their central point but 130 may indicate rather higher ability on some scales than others.

On the Continent there are, generally speaking, no intelligence tests, but attainment tests are set nationally, regionally or

---

[1] The Scottish average is in the region of 30-35 per cent, often reaching 40 per cent and exceptionally 50 per cent or more. The English average is in the region of 15-25 per cent exceptionally reaching 40 per cent: but in areas where only 15 per cent or less enter Grammar Schools, there are often several Secondary Modern Schools with an academic " side ".

locally, in all the main subjects of the curriculum. In Norway the class teacher's report alone is considered and this is apt to give rather subjective results. Pupils from very small schools are often over-assessed because the teacher has not, for some years, encountered any who were of really high ability. About a tenth of those admitted to the *realskola* therefore drop out after a year and are replaced by continuation class (eighth-year primary) pupils who take an entrance examination set by the secondary school.

There might be a strong case for attainment tests in subjects other than Arithmetic and English as part of our selection procedure—they would help to find out the pupil with a special interest in geography, history or natural science and would give him more scope to express himself than standardized English tests, this giving some indication also of his ability in English.

In Scotland, as throughout Western Europe, middle class pupils have a much greater chance of passing into academic streams or schools than pupils from working-class families. Their parents provide more books, more conversation of a cultivated kind, better facilities for homework and above all a much stronger incentive to get on, since maintenance of the standard of living and the way of life they know depends on their being placed in a five-year course and taking the necessary examinations and qualifications thereafter. Furthermore middle-class parents are probably more aware that an *appeal* procedure exists, for those who have marginally "failed" the transfer examination, and more ready to take advantage of it, going on if need be to the Secretary of State.

As often as not, pupils whose parents appeal are then placed in an academic school or stream, since there are plenty of places available, and it is easy enough to "demote" them later if they are clearly out of their depth. "Appeal" pupils usually manage to stay in the academic course, however, since they and their parents tend to show more than average determination to make up for their lack of measured ability.

The early wastage among "academic" pupils is more likely to affect working-class boys and girls, placed in the five-year course because of their good showing in the transfer examination, but not very determined and insufficiently backed (or sometimes actually thwarted) by their parents. This fact has also been observed in Germany and Holland. It is a risk attendant on free or nearly free secondary "grammar" education; where fees are payable all parents, and especially those of limited means, will think twice before letting their children embark on the course and thrice before letting them drop out prematurely. But, where fees are high enough to keep the wastage down, they are also high enough to keep out pupils who could and would have completed the course.

The secondary course is shorter in Scotland than almost anywhere else, because of the relatively high transfer age. But one must remember that in most Western European countries many pupils remain in a primary school throughout,[1] with perhaps a continuation class or course at the end, while in Eastern Europe the primary-secondary school usually forms an undivided whole, with "secondary" subjects and specialist teachers appearing gradually from the fifth year onwards.

We differ from England not only in transferring pupils a year later but in putting twice as many of them into the "academic" course. The initial wastage is higher, and more pupils leave without any certificate, but of those who stay on, more have, till now, qualified to enter universities. In consequence the ratio of students to the total population is about 1 in 250 here, but 1 in 400 across the Border. If all the Scottish students in England (mainly Oxford and Cambridge undergraduates) were exchanged for all the English here—mainly "Oxbrige" rejects who are unwilling to demean themselves by entering a "Redbrick", the proportions might work out at 1 in 280 and 1 in 390 respectively, still giving us a very substantial advantage—though one should remember that our standard honours course lasts four years while in Oxford and Cambridge at least, with a more selective entry, it often lasts three years only.

On the other hand a higher proportion of English pupils learn a language other than their own—nearly all do so in technical schools or streams and in the "A" stream of some

[1] It should be observed that "primary school" and approximately equivalent terms (Ecole Primaire, Volkschule, Folkskola, etc.) do not mean the same in all Western European countries. The objective is merely the achievement of basic literacy in some of them (e.g. Spain, Portugal) while in others it includes everything locally expected of the intelligent but not intellectual citizen, including the beginnings of a foreign language (Germany, Sweden). Sometimes the course ends early for all (e.g. at 11 in Portugal) sometimes late for all (14 in Norway): more often the pupils of presumed "grammar ability" are creamed off at ages ranging from 10 to 13, while the average and below-average stay on to the end of compulsory schooling at 14 or 15.

Secondary Modern schools: many in the "B" stream of Secondary Modern schools also.

The proportion of pupils embarking on the academic course here is much the same (30 to 35 per cent) as in Germany and Southern Scandinavia. In Northern Scandinavia it is much higher, reaching 90% and above in a few towns near or beyond the Arctic Circle (Haparanda, Kiruna, Hammerfest). In France and in Central Europe it is difficult to establish as there often exists a highly academic school (gymnasium) and a moderately academic school (e.g. the Swiss general secondary school) between them educating a majority of pupils, while a less able minority complete their formal education in the primary school. In Southern Europe, 10% or less start on the academic course, but nearly all the "starters" complete it, and this causes quite serious middle-class unemployment or under-employment in Greece, Spain and Southern Italy.

On the Continent, however, a much higher proportion of all pupils, whether academic or non-academic, start on a foreign language or on the second language of their own country if it happens to have one. In Scandinavia even the equivalents of our "Modifieds" have a shot at English. In Germany all but the bottom 20% or so make a start on English—or on French in areas adjoining France. The same is true of the Netherlands —the language being English in the two provinces of Holland proper, but sometimes German in the Eastern border areas. In France again all those who get as far as the Cours Complémentaire (roughly our Junior Secondary minus its "Modified" and some of its "practical" pupils) learn English, or the nearest foreign language in certain border areas. In Switzerland nearly all learn a second national language in the top classes of the primary school (i.e. at ages 13-14) and all learn it, as well as a third language[1] or alternatively English, in the corresponding classes of the general secondary school. In Russia all must take

[1] Switzerland has four national languages. Only one is purely Swiss—Romansch, used by 1 per cent of the population. The others are German (69 per cent) French (21 per cent) and Italian (9 per cent). But most of those who *write* German speak "Switzertütsch" which differs from it as much as Scots from Standard English, and is increasingly being used on occasions when Scots would hardly ever be used here.

The Suisses-Romands speak standard French but with some distinctive usages (cf. "outwith" and "do you wish soup?" in Edinburgh Standard English). Thus 70, 80 and 90 in Geneva—as in Brussels—are "*septante*" "*huitante*" *and* "*nonante*" instead of *soixante-dix*, *quatre-vingt* and *quatre-vingt-dix* and are taught as such in the schools.

a language from the sixth school year upwards—most schools have English but some have French, German or a non-European language, e.g. Arabic or Chinese. In most other Communist countries Russian usually appears in the fifth or sixth year and is again compulsory for all: in Yugoslavia there is a choice as in Russia, many schools having English, others German, French, Russian or even Latin.

The only remaining European countries in which a substantial proportion of all pupils never make a start on any foreign language are Ireland (because of the excessive time given to Irish, a dwindling minority language), England (mainly because of her insular traditions), Portugal, Spain, Italy, Greece and Turkey (all with high rates of illiteracy in some regions at least). This puts us in very disreputable company, the more so since Italy is trying hard to pull out and meet the standards of her Common Market colleagues.

My own view is that all secondary pupils should at least try to learn a " foreign " language unless clearly incapable of even making a start—and I am not enough of a Nationalist to regard English as " foreign " in that sense. But this language need not be French nor need it always be taught in the way one usually teaches a foreign language to academic pupils. There is a strong case for Norwegian, Swedish and Spanish as alternatives.[1]

Spanish is the easiest to learn of the major foreign languages and is more widely spoken abroad than French.

Norwegian and Swedish are very easy to learn, at least in an approximate way (and one cannot expect more of non-academic pupils) once one has got used to the idea that they have the definite article at the end, in a slightly different form for words of the common and neuter genders respectively. They have many words found, slightly altered, in Scottish and Northumbrian English—e.g. " bairn ", to " greet " (in the sense of " weep ") " braw ", " gate " (in the sense of " street "), " fell " in names of mountains or mountainous areas, and a whole host

---

[1] This raises certain staffing problems. In the first instance, considerable use would have to be made of temporary assistants (largely Modern Languages students) from Norway, Sweden and Spain, and summer courses would have to be organised for them, to give them a basic idea of educational methods before letting them loose on our schools. Subsequently one would try to encourage Scottish students, with a permanent or temporary teaching career in mind, to study one of these languages as part of their Ordinary degree course.

of words in common with standard English as they stand or altered but easily recognised.

Learning a language, even with limited success, does three things, even for the pupil of limited ability, and perhaps especially for him.

(1) It makes him feel more "secondary" and increases his self-respect.

(2) It helps him to realise that there are other ways of thinking, feeling and expressing oneself than his own, and thus broadens his mind and his outlook.

(3) It gives him an added interest, or helps to start an interest not sufficiently awakened by his geography teacher, in other peoples and their surroundings and way of life.

It also helps to fill out his time-table; with eight or nine periods of English a week the law of diminishing returns begins to operate, and in any case the process of learning a foreign language is often a help to that of improving one's own.

My own view is that the teaching of these languages should probably start in P.VI or P.VII, at least for the abler pupil, and in S.I for the rest, or possibly S.II, since it is at this stage that the non-academic pupil begins to get bored with the apparent futility of school work.

As regards other subjects the only ones on which I have strong views are History, English and Latin.

It seems to me fantastic that Scottish pupils should be able to pass "Ordinary" and "Higher" Grade History without answering a single Scottish question. English pupils could not get away with no English history at the Ordinary or the Advanced Level. Scottish history does not stop at 1707 or even 1745 as teachers and textbooks only too often assume. It also includes a considerable slice of the Industrial Revolution, which came to us later than to England and in a somewhat different form—the tremendous Scottish contribution to Imperial history, especially in the exploration of Africa and the settlement of Canada and New Zealand—and a study of the ways in which Scotland remains different from England and of the causes and effects of this difference. But perhaps it is contrary to public policy that Scots lads and lasses should take too great a pride in their own country, in so far as it remains distinct from the greater whole with which it has been partly merged.

English is too often heaped upon teachers of anything and everything to fill out their time-table, especially if their normal subject is one for which there is a limited demand—for instance French in the academic stream of a junior secondary school. It is also used to fill out the time-table of non-academic pupils in defiance of the law of diminishing returns, whereby more than six periods a week of anything is probably too much. It is often taught to non-academic pupils by teachers essentially appointed for their ability to teach the academic ones and for their interest in this admittedly large and important minority.

Though not a "foreign" language except in the Gaelic-speaking areas, English is not exactly the mother-tongue of all pupils. Scots as spoken in the home is much more different from the "official standard" than are many of the Southern working-class dialects and ways of speech (you cannot really call what is spoken in South and East London a "dialect" but it is not standard English.)

This is an advantage in some ways: in particular the attainment of "practical" stream pupils here, in grammar and spelling, is probably higher than that of the corresponding English youngsters in the B stream of a Secondary Modern School, though their vocabulary may be more limited. It is easier to teach the correct spelling, pronunciation and use of any given word to a pupil who uses a quite different word at home, than to one who habitually misuses the same word.

But there are also certain difficulties not arising in England, and these mainly concern pronunciation and usage. What should be taught as correct English: the language as spoken by an educated Londoner, and specifically a news announcer at Broadcasting House, or as spoken by someone who has completed the course of a fee-paying day school in Edinburgh? I personally use the Broadcasting House Dialect, because I was mainly educated in England, but regard Edinburgh Standard as correct in this country and generally follow the distinctive Scottish usage where there is one (e.g. "outwith" instead of "outside" as a preposition.) Others are less sure and London usage is encroaching all the time, especially between Forth and Tweed.

How, for instance, would you pronounce "Angela Annan" if you had a pupil of that name? I think I should make a clean break between the forename and the surname, but quite a few people would put in an "r" for euphony, as any Londoner would.

If you were teaching French (to which some English is incidental, as to all other subjects) how would you tell the

75

pupils to translate "ruisseau"? I would commend the native "burn", allow the neutral "stream" but firmly score out the alien "brook".

As to Latin the main difficulty is that it does not lend itself to co-educational teaching. Most of the older textbooks — especially the *Hillard and Botting—North and Hillard* combination are quite unmistakeably designed by men for boys, and so is most of Latin literature itself. The textbooks designed to appeal to girls or to mixed classes look very "cissy" to boys: the only satisfactory solution is to use group methods and have one set of books for boys and another for girls.

My principal quarrel, however, is not with the teaching of this or that subject but with the organisation and timing of the secondary curriculum as a whole.

There is no doubt that Scottish primary pupils are more thoroughly grounded, at the time of transferring to a secondary school or department, than pupils in most other European countries, including England. This is partly due to the greater length of the primary course, partly to the personality of the teachers and the methods employed, partly to the high regard in which education is generally held and the consequent willingness of parents to co-operate with the school.

But the ablest pupils are frustrated by having to follow a primary curriculum and remain under a class teacher for a year and perhaps two years longer than is necessary. They then have to make up for time wasted by cramming the secondary course into five years where most countries have six, seven or eight, while other pupils "academic" but not brilliant, have to try and keep up with them. At this stage the curriculum and the pace are timed for the best while in the primary school they are set for the reasonably good.

At the top end there is a lack of liaison with the Universities. In the past these were prepared to complete the work of small, under-staffed and under-equipped parish schools; now their arrangements assume an efficient all-round secondary education, ability, on the student's part to work on his own for much of the time, and readiness to work without immediate compulsion. The schools have concentrated on the all-round secondary education at the expense of the other two main requirements.

This is a fault common to secondary schools throughout Europe, with the sole exception of England—though some of the blame also attaches to the University staff—again throughout

Europe except at Oxford, Cambridge and Dublin (Trinity College)—for taking too little personal interest in the students especially in their first year.

Perhaps the simplest way to consider how well or badly our children and adolescents are educated is to divide them into six approximate intellectual categories and compare what is done for these categories here, in England, and in a few other European countries.

My categories are (and it must be remembered that all approximations are to some extent misleading): [1]

A *Highly academic pupils*, eventually capable of honours degree without undue expenditure of effort. The rare *geniuses* form a subdivision " A plus " within this category.

B *Academic* pupils likely to last the five-year course. Most should take " Highers ": many will take ordinary degrees, a few, with a really sustained effort, will manage an honours degree.

C *Moderately Academic* pupils, likely to start on the five-year course, whether language or technical, but generally unlikely to complete it, unless their determination and parental backing more than make up for their comparative lack of ability. The new " Ordinary Grade " will be a reasonable though fairly ambitious goal for such pupils.

D *Average* pupils—roughly speaking the better two-thirds of those starting on the three-year course.

E *Sub-Average* pupils of the type normally found in " Modified " streams here and in the C and D streams of Secondary Modern schools in England.

F *Educationally sub-normal* pupils who must or should attend a " special school ".

Only a fairly large and prosperous local authority can do much for pupils in Category F, and such authorities are more numerous in England than here. For this reason I think such pupils are likely to be catered for much more generously in England than here, but I cannot claim personal experience of them.

Category E. Here I stand on more familiar ground, having taught these pupils in both countries and met them abroad.

---

[1] These categories cannot be stated accurately in terms of I.Q's since other factors, especially the pupils' own determination, parental backing and previous grounding must be all taken into consideration. Other things being equal, on Moray House scales, I would suggest 125 approx. as the lower limit for Category A, 115 for Category B, 105 for Category C, 90 for Category D and 75 for Category E.

We compare badly with England for three reasons at least.

(a) In England they will be in Secondary Modern Schools on which a great deal of money has been spent, and where they will be with teachers of whom a fair proportion are interested in teaching non-academic pupils, but whose spirits are kept up by having a few semi-academic ones.

In Scotland they may be found in junior secondary schools or in the bottom stream of a senior secondary or omnibus school. Junior secondary schools *pure and simple* are not places where most teachers want to teach, since they exclude the best 35% rather than the best 15% of all pupils. In Senior Secondary and Omnibus schools most of the staff, other than those teaching "practical" subjects, are appointed mainly to teach the academic pupils. They will take the "Modifieds" if need be, because it is part of their job, but without the personal interest and fellow feeling which they reserve for their academic and semi-academic pupils and for the few "highly academic" who come their way.

(b) Where the "Modifieds" are in a school which also has pupils belonging to categories A, B and C they will often find the curriculum and time-table are planned largely in terms of these pupils.[1] It therefore becomes impossible to organise projects and expeditions as they can be organised in a purely non-academic school, since the teachers who could run this kind of "show" are in fact required at certain set times to teach academic subjects to academic pupils.

The English Secondary Modern School, if it has an imaginative headmaster and staff, and any necessary financial backing from the local education authority, can do more along these lines than most secondary schools in Scotland; furthermore the looser structure of the educational system in England allows greater freedom to such a headmaster and staff.[2]

(c) Since there are nine times as many pupils in England as in Scotland, educational publishing is more worthwhile south of the border—though several great educational publishers are "amphibious" and originally Scottish firms. This means more scope for experiment, since with half-a-dozen steady best-sellers on his back list a publisher can afford to take twenty or thirty uncertain risks. Hence there is a greater choice of interesting

---

[1] This depends on local circumstances: more can be done for "Modified" pupils in large towns.

[2] See *Kneebone*, "I Teach in a Secondary Modern School" (Routledge & Kegan Paul, 1957).

text-books in all subjects for pupils of this type and of Category D.

Actually no country has really worked out what should be done with such pupils, either in terms of objectives or of courses. The Russians are probably groping in the right direction by making more room for practical work *on a worthwhile scale* and by the friendly and mutually beneficial association of certain schools with certain factories and farms. (see *Schools of Europe*, Chapter II).

But they spoil much of the good effect by a determined refusal to " stream " pupils in class time. This means overtime remedial work for the less able, since all follow a curriculum designed for pupils in Category C.[1]

Category D. Here again we compare unfavourably with England, but these pupils at least are not completely out of their depth. All three reasons given above again help to explain our relative inferiority, but there is also a fourth. In England such pupils would normally be among the decent average or better ones in a school designed for them, and would have every chance of becoming prefects and members of the usual school teams. Here they will have the same opportunities in a *purely* junior secondary school, and in a small omnibus school whose brighter pupils move on at 14 to a senior secondary school. But as non-academic pupils in a senior secondary or large omnibus school they will be at the same disadvantage as in an English multilateral or comprehensive school—they will be crowded out by the academic and highly academic pupils.

English local authorities, owing to their greater resources, can again put on a greater variety of curricula for Category D pupils; but they probably fare best in the Netherlands and in Switzerland, where most of them will find their way to schools designed for themselves and for most of the pupils belonging to Category C. This however is done at the expense of Category E who find themselves in schools and classes that are definitely " the end ".

Category C. Here we begin to come into our own. Most such pupils, if English, go into a Secondary Modern School where they start with a sense of failure but may recover if the

---

[1] It also means " voluntary overtime " by A and some B pupils in more advanced groups, meeting outwith school hours. Participation in such groups is a more or less necessary condition of university entrance for senior pupils and of promotion to headships for ambitious teachers.

school has a certificate " side ", as an increasing number of them have. But such pupils, if at all numerous in a Secondary Modern School, are a temptation to its staff to neglect categories D and E, though they are useful as leaven and as an attraction to competent teachers.

In Scotland Category C pupils go into an academic school or stream and are put on their mettle. If they have average or above-average determination they will make good use of the opportunities which would not have been theirs in England. Since the primary curriculum is *planned* and *timed* for them they benefit from a grounding which is second to none and equalled only by the Dutch, the Scandinavians and possibly the Swiss.

A small sub-category "C plus", probably do better in England—they are the pupils who would just have got into a Grammar School, where they would not be distracted by the presence of friends intending to leave at the minimum age.

Actually Category C pupils are those who benefit most from being sent to a fee-paying school, if they can get in, since this is where they will find the atmosphere most conducive to hard, steady work.

This category of pupils, again, probably get the best education in Switzerland and in Germany where there are secondary schools explicitly designed for them and known as *Sekundar-schulen* and *Realschulen* respectively.

Category B. Here Scotland is not merely superior but supreme. Pupils in this category are perhaps a little better than their school, but not so much that their last year's work is wasted. At the secondary level they find a curriculum planned and timed for them from start to finish, with an objective ambitious, as it should be, but not beyond their reach.

For such pupils, the Scottish " Highers " form a far more satisfactory climax to their school career than the English " A " levels, because they do not allow them to relapse into ignorance of any major subject but demand a consistent though not super-human effort on a broad front.

I feel, however, that " B " pupils going on to Universities should be encouraged to do a sixth year at school wherever possible, and taught, with some at least of their " Highers " safely behind them, to work under semi-student conditions. This would reduce the wastage of good material later.

Alternatively it should become standard procedure for all

such pupils to take a fair range of " Ordinary Grades " in their fourth year and then spend a *further two years* preparing for " Highers ". These would continue to be taken on a broad front but the nature of the papers should be changed, not by demanding *more knowledge* but by requiring more evidence of *thought* and of *appropriate general reading* and a decidedly higher standard of English composition not only in English but in all subjects requiring the use of continuous prose (i.e. Classics, Modern Languages, History, Geography and to some extent Science).

One or two *oral tests* could be added, as in Scandinavia, mainly to test general culture and reasoning ability, and these tests should be conducted by persons with some experience of full-time or part-time University teaching.

Category A and sub-category A-plus. Here, in motor-cycle parlance, we are definitely past the peak of our power curve. We compare badly not only with England but with all those countries in which academic and highly academic pupils transfer at 10 or 11 and enter schools in which the non-academic have no place.

A and *A-plus* pupils start with a wasted year behind them. They continue to waste time for two or three years until many or most of the *C* pupils have dropped out altogether or fallen back into a stream catering only for Ordinary Grade candidates (hitherto " Lower Leavings"). Thereafter they set the pace, and take all the necessary examinations in their stride. But, outwith the official curriculum, they miss a great deal which they would probably have picked up in England, France or Germany. The time they have wasted means less remains for general reading and indeed for reading directly connected with their subject. This weakness is especially felt in those subjects which require a good deal of such reading, notably History and French.

They should not be pitied excessively—at least they achieve their objectives, but these objectives can and must be made more challenging and worthwhile, and this presupposes a reform of the senior secondary curriculum in so far as they are involved.

A-plus pupils are difficult to cater for. To my knowledge only half-a-dozen schools, all in England, give them what I would regard as a satisfactory education. *Winchester* is actually designed for them or at least has a stream designed for them as do *Manchester Grammar School* and one or two other large day schools. *Eton* is big enough to have such a stream, and houses them in a little community within the community; this is traditional but perhaps not the best for them. *Millfield* is expensive enough to provide them with special tuition in small groups, and unlike the others, can lay something on for the boy who is a genius in some directions but not others. *Harrow* makes no special arrangements but such a boy is normally recognised for what he is and allowed to work on his own with a selection of the finest textbooks in every subject. Furthermore masters are normally willing to spend quite a lot of their spare time with him, and this, rather than special arrangements involving some form of intellectual segregation, is probably the ideal way to educate him. It presupposes either the atmosphere of a boarding school, where the extra time is readily found and if necessary made. or day school teachers of more than average ability and willingness to help.

Probably the simplest way to deal with such pupils would be for the Scottish Education Department to buy places for them at preparatory schools, or the primary departments of fee-paying secondary schools, and at corresponding " Public " and Grant-Aided schools thereafter. They are an embarrassment to the primary and secondary schools where they find themselves, since the genius only stimulates those who, though within the normal range of ability, are well above average themselves— with the rest he has no real point of contact. I am fairly sure the independent and grant-aided schools concerned would be only too willing to co-operate. An alternative, if they were unable or reluctant, would be to set up an experimental school containing a substantial proportion of geniuses but enough other Category A pupils to prevent it from developing too rarified and unnatural an atmosphere.[1]

But this particular problem is on a very small scale, and reform of the educational arrangements for Category A pupils generally would be more to the point.

At the *primary* level I think we should consider for such pupils: —

(a) Earlier transfer either to S.I or to a preliminary class attached to a secondary school or department, having a class

[1] This could be best done, on a grant-aided basis, by a voluntary body such as *Mensa*, acting together with the University Departments of Education. One such school could reasonably be situated in each University town. To help fill up the school and so cut overheads per pupil, English pupils of similar calibre might be admitted, and arrangements made for them to board with the parents of local " A plus " pupils.

teacher for much of the time (e.g. in English, History, Religious Instruction and French or Geography).

(b) The teaching of some secondary subjects in P.VII A and P.VI A, where the top primary classes are streamed. French and General Science would be the obvious choices: the teachers for these subjects would be "borrowed" from the secondary school or department nearby, or the class teacher would take them but some other teacher would then relieve him of that class in some other subject. I feel the transition from class to subject teaching ought, and not only for these pupils, to be made more gradual than it is at present. Ideally the pupil should meet two teachers of academic subjects in P.VI, three in P.VII, four or five in S.I and the full range, whatever it is, only in S.II.

(c) The setting up of a rather better A stream in P.VI and P.VII at some centrally placed schools. This would retain its primary atmosphere—with mainly but not exclusively class teaching, while an enriched curriculum, with one or two additional subjects, and a different approach in the regular "primary" ones, could be introduced. This experiment has been carried on for some years, with reasonable success, in a number of East German schools, and the fee-paying primary classes of grant-aided and some public secondary schools are, in effect, units of this type.

At the secondary level the main consideration is that the teachers must retain and replenish not only their knowledge but their interest in their work. It is no good having Category A pupils taught French by someone who has not been to France for the past five years and never reads a modern French book for *enjoyment*, or Classics by one who has never stood in the Coliseum with the memories of Emperors, gladiators and martyrs surging all around him, or on Cape Sunium's "marbled steep" to watch the sun rising or setting on the Isles of Greece. Nor should they be taught history by one to whom Alexander, Charlemagne, Luther and Napoleon are names and bundles of facts and dates, rather than living personalities and the embodiment as well as the shapers of a nation and of an age.

Near the end of the secondary course I have already indicated my feeling that there should be more definite preparation for the *atmosphere* as well as the *nature* and *scope* of University work, and this should be done mainly in the sixth

SCHOOLS OF SCOTLAND

year of the course, and the seventh for those who start a year early.

This should tie up with a reform of university arrangements allowing of a three-years Honours course (as in England) for those who complete seven years at a secondary school and for the best of those who complete six years. They could qualify for this by taking the normal first-year University examinations or an agreed equivalent while still at school. This would set free a useful number of places at the Universities. I am *not* in favour of the first year of the ordinary degree course being by-passed in this way since I believe it is a mistake and a waste of wonderful time to spend *less* than three years at a University if one goes up at all.

Two more reforms are in my opinion imperative, one in the existing academic course and the other in the whole set-up of non-academic education.

1. I am strongly opposed to the present arrangement whereby many small burgh schools (e.g. Jedburgh Grammar) lose their best pupils after two years. This discourages teachers from joining their staffs, especially in subjects for which a demand remains but is greatly reduced by this early transfer of academic pupils to a larger school. At the same time it diminishes the reputation of the school and incidentally of the small burgh itself.[1]

Such schools should be allowed to retain their academic pupils up to the new Ordinary Grade, and these pupils should then have the possibility of going into the *preparatory department* of a University and working there under semi-student conditions for the University Preliminary Examination which is a fair and in some ways more interesting equivalent of "Highers" (it includes a possible choice of most European and some non-European languages, for instance).

In the second year of their preparatory course they would be joined by students from schools running a five-year course but too small to have a sixth year, and possibly by students from schools with a sixth year, but for whom a preparatory year was

[1] One of my critics has observed at this point " this ignores the scarcity of educated manpower ".

While there is a valid practical argument for " rationalisation " one must remember that a school with an academic stream needs a teacher for languages. If the academic pupils move on after two years he cannot be employed full-time in his proper capacity.

I stand by my opinion that, if a school has an academic stream, the pupils in it should remain up to the new " Ordinary Grade ".

84

thought more suitable (not every 17-year-old still fits into the pattern of *school* life, but he may not be quite ready for University work.) At the end of the preparatory course they would meet students with six years' secondary schooling behind them, in the first year of the ordinary degree or four year Honours course.

This arrangement, beside improving the atmosphere and staffing situation of small burgh schools, would restore to them the prestige of being institutions from which one can proceed straight to University. It would also remove the temptation, for some pupils—not all of them "marginal" as regards ability —to drop out of the academic course at the end of the second year, and thus avoid a longish daily journey, boarding away from home, or a parting from their non-academic friends. At the end of their fourth year such pupils may be better placed to decide—if the question arises—whether it is worth their while going on.

(2) As I have indicated the aims and curriculum of "junior secondary" education ought to be reconsidered and overhauled. It is not just a question of finding a new and less humiliating name: the thing itself needs to be transformed. The people who plan education usually belong to intellectual Category A. They have never known what it is to be in Categories D and E and may not have recent experience of teaching such pupils, whose character and limitations are soon forgotten, when one loses close and almost daily contact with them.

One of these limitations is that they cannot sit still and be quiet for any length of time. They have restless minds and emotions in bodies far larger than those of their parents at the same age. Fear will not hold them down: they are nearly if not quite as big and strong as most of their teachers, at any rate in S.III. The problem will of course be even graver if the leaving age is raised to 16 before anybody has worked out what is to be done with the extra year and with the year added in 1945.

Not in jest but in full and deadly earnest I should like to make a constructive suggestion.

Next time a Working Party is appointed to report on Junior Secondary Education, let four junior secondary pupils be co-opted —a boy and a girl each from town and country, awake but not academic, intelligent but not bookish. They will not waste more time by attending its deliberations than they would probably have wasted in school, and indeed it may do them some good to sit among the doctors and professors. To these doctors and professors they will be a permanent reminder and a living reference-book in four parts, and they may even make some useful contribution in their own right—simply by explaining as best they can what they would like to learn and how they would like to learn it.

There is nothing to be lost by giving them their chance.

Has anybody who plans education as a whole thought what it feels like to be a lad of 14 and three-quarters, approaching six feet and twelve stone, tied to a desk for most of the time from 9 till 12 and 1-15 till 4, doing things which are not going to be the slightest use to oneself six months hence, with a birthday in early September and waiting for Christmas, enviously thinking of those who were born in mid-August and need not sit through next term?

Has anybody who lays down curricula found time to run through a few of the paltry "readers" designed for the children of another generation and still expected to satisfy the adolescents of today? What is the use of a couple of paragraphs from an insipid fairy tale, with a comprehension test and a few additional exercises, to a 13-year-old, ungrammatical but not illiterate and moving in the divided world of East and West, the spinning space-ships and the dark flames of the African revolt?

CHAPTER V

The Grant-Aided and Independent Schools

Though relatively fewer than in England, the Scottish Grant-Aided and Independent Schools are certainly important enough to deserve a chapter to themselves. Together they educate only 3% of the population, as against 7% in England and well over half in some Continental countries. But this 3% includes most of those who could be described as the upper middle class and in particular, a high proportion of those who plan, direct and administer education in this country.

I cannot compete with Curtis, Knox and Strong, among others, in giving the history of these schools. A few details must suffice here to explain how they came into being and why, until the present century, they have formed a less significant part of the educational picture than in England, France or Holland for instance.

At the time of the Reformation Scotland, although poorer in other respects, had a better network of schools than England: the Reformers were decidedly " school-friendly " and improved the network so far that it remained for generations the finest in Europe.

The poverty of the Church had brought pre-Reformation burgh schools under municipal control, so they did not perish with the abbeys and priories as so many perished in England about 1535-40. Consequently there was no need for people like Judd, Sheriff and Lyon (the founders of Tonbridge, Rugby, Harrow). Nor, due to the poverty of the country itself, were there such people at the time. What the Reformers did was to create or revive hundreds of parish schools, thus narrowing the educational gap between town and country.

Until the eighteenth century public day schools — often protected by municipal by-laws—had a virtual monopoly of all but the most elementary education, as they have over the greater part of Scandinavia to this day.

With greater prosperity individual or corporate endowment became possible. Corporate endowment came first, in the Merchant Company "Hospitals" (c. 1760).[1] At the time these closely resembled Christ's Hospital in London, in that extreme poverty was the main qualification for entry and that they were *welfare institutions* as much as *educational establishments*.

The individual foundations — e.g. the present Dollar Academy, Madras College and Bell-Baxter High School—were purely "educational" from the start (Madras and Bell-Baxter have since come under Local Authority control).

In 1868-69 some of these schools, and in 1872-75 all of them, were investigated by Royal Commissions. The recommendations of the second commission are outlined in detail by H. M. Knox in 250 *Years of Scottish Education*, Chapter V. The outcome was that the welfare and educational elements in these foundations were "unscrambled", and they became fee-paying day schools of somewhat higher calibre than the average run of secondary schools. The "foundationers" (pupils cared for as well as educated free or at very low cost) were boarded out and generally sent to public elementary schools in the first instance.

The "English-type" boarding schools had a somewhat different early history. Most of them were founded in the middle of the nineteenth century or later, and by the combined effort of a number of generous and public-spirited individuals: Fettes alone by individual bequest. They were never closely associated with the existing educational system as the grant-aided day schools were—though perhaps less distant than in England since they have always taken a fairly large proportion of their pupils from "State" schools. Their appearance was resented by many, and even now educated public opinion is not fully reconciled to their presence. Hostility towards them does not take quite the same form as in England: there they are disliked for being "upper-class" and hotbeds of prejudice and privilege—here mainly for being English in organisation and outlook.

At the moment, however, they seem to be increasing in strength and prestige. The number of pupils who attend them

---

[1] George Heriot's (Edinburgh) is actually 130 years older, and an individual foundation, but was for generations alone of its kind.

is subject to some fluctuation, if the statistics are to be believed. But this fluctuation is somewhat misleading. It occurs because some independent schools may become grant-aided, while others appear or disappear, and while grant-aided schools occasionally surrender to local authority control.

The *main* trend, in Southern Scotland at least, is quite unmistakeable: the best independent schools are capturing pupils from the grant-aided schools which recoup themselves at the expense of public secondary schools. At the same time fee-paying primary departments, where they exist, and preparatory schools, are capturing middle-class pupils from primary schools. Why is this happening?

One reason, certainly, is the pervasive spread of English influence. The middle class generally read one or more of the three English Sunday papers which cater for their tastes, there being no corresponding Scottish paper as yet. Many of them— perhaps as many as half, read an English daily paper. Through these papers and the subtle, possibly unconscious persuasion of their English friends, they come to regard an independent education as the norm for children of their class.

Another reason, probably more important, is the real or supposed decline in the quality of public education. *So far as the middle class are concerned* I think the decline is real enough. In their efforts to provide a better all-round education (including much " educational welfare ") for the many, the authorities have neglected the special requirements of the few.[1]

Parents who can give their children attractive home surroundings, adequate facilities for homework, holidays in some new and exciting place every year, and a fairly high standard of culture all round are not interested in all the amenities which are now being laid on, to broaden and enrich the life of the 80%.

What they want is that the schools should do their traditional job effectively, and never mind about the rest. They want first-rate teachers putting across sound learning, working their children hard and keeping them well under control. They demand an atmosphere in which all are pressing at a resolute and consistent pace towards well-defined objectives — in this

---

[1] This may seem to contradict some of what I said in the previous chapter. Undoubtedly *some* thought has gone into what should be done with less academic pupils. But dilution of academic content *plus* project methods *plus* educational welfare are not necessarily the answer.

instance " Highers" and the Open Bursary Competition. These are the objectives for *their* children and they are not interested in other people's children for whom these objectives are too ambitious or the pace too fast.

Public Secondary Schools are taking more account of "the many's" requirements than formerly, and that is as it should be. But, in doing this, they have become less challenging to " the few", and less acceptable to their parents (and to parents who believe their children to be among "the few").

Another reason, in some areas, may be the policy of "rationalisation". A small burgh school which loses its senior pupils to a larger school ten or twenty miles away loses with them its spirit, its pride and its self-respect. The local doctor and lawyer, educated there themselves, see no cause to carry on the family tradition only to break it as their sons and daughters enter S.III and Certificate work starts in earnest. So they make an arrangement with a brother or uncle in Edinburgh and send them to one of the Merchant Company Schools or—if their means allows it—they forsake the Scottish system altogether and enter them for a boarding school.

The grant-aided schools, for historical reasons, dominate " the educational picture " in Edinburgh.[1] They also exist in Glasgow, Dundee, Aberdeen and a few other towns, in some of which (e.g. Crieff) they happen to be the only senior secondary school.

They differ from public senior secondary schools in the following respects.

(a) They are independently managed by a Board of Governors who appoint the Headmaster and normally leave him free to appoint his staff. But the Local Authority may be represented on the Board, and the Governors may " vet " and possibly veto senior appointments.

(b) They normally have no " non-certificate " pupils. They usually set their own entrance examination, of a higher standard than the normal " transfer exam " or " qualifying " but may be required, as a condition of their grant, to admit Local Authority pupils on the " qualifying " rather than on their own examination.

(c) They have discretionary powers of refusing pupils on other than academic grounds (viz. general " unsuitability ") and of suspending and expelling trouble-makers.

[1] See appendix J (page 187).

(d) All except Marr College, Troon, charge fees.

(e) Nearly all are single-sex.

(f) Some have primary departments, also fee-charging, with a curriculum differing in some respects from that of public primary schools and departments—e.g. by introducing French in P.IV or thereabouts. Such departments are also annexed to a few public senior secondary schools, e.g. Aberdeen Grammar School.

(g) They have a slightly better staffing ratio, and on an average, better staff. This is not due to their paying higher salaries—as a rule they don't except in so far as there may be more posts of responsibility with better allowances—but to their existing status, to the many advantages inherent in *not* being subject to an Education Committee and above all to the absence of non-academic or socially very undesirable pupils.

Their points of contact with the public educational system are as follows: —

(i) They exist mainly on public funds—that is on grants from the Scottish Education Department. Since the proportion of pupils over 16, for whom a double grant is payable, is far higher than in any public day schools, they may in some cases have more public money spent on them per pupil—or at any rate more S.E.D. money, than senior secondary schools of corresponding size.

(ii) As a counterpart of their grant they are conducted in accordance with the Schools (Scotland) Code. This implies that their staff have Scottish rather than English qualifications— except in so far as they may receive " exceptional recognition " from the S.E.D. and that their pupils work towards Scottish rather than English examinations. In consequence these pupils normally go on to Scottish Universities.

(iii) A further condition of their grant is that 50% of their pupils must come from public primary schools.[1] In fact most of the remaining 50% also come from primary schools, though possibly spending some years in the fee-paying primary department. They may for instance attend a public infant department and join the fee-paying primary department at P.III or P.IV.

(iv) The Headmasters of these schools meet other Senior

---

[1] This rule does not apply in every case. It is mainly found where the grant-aided school happens to be the only senior secondary school in its town (e.g. Dollar, Crieff).

Secondary Headmasters regularly in the Scottish Senior Secondary Headmasters Association. The Heads of the Independent Schools also belong but attend less frequently (except the Headmaster of Fort Augustus, which enters boys for Scottish rather than English examinations).

(v) They are nearly all Day Schools: a few have a Boarding department.

In their status, atmosphere and purposes these schools are very similar to the English Direct Grant Schools, with certain important differences nevertheless. Thus the Direct Grant Schools send their better pupils into Oxford or Cambridge and their " ordinary degree material " to the Redbricks, thus getting up to 80% of all their pupils into a University. Some of our grant-aided schools also reach this very high figure, but send all or nearly all their University entrants to Scottish Universities, whatever their weaknesses or their strength. The Direct Grant Schools are also, in some places (e.g. Manchester, Birmingham, Bradford) in a stronger position than any corresponding school in Scotland. Finally whereas the Grant-Aided School Headmasters, whether or not they are also members of the H.M.C., mainly associate with other Secondary School Headmasters, the Direct Grant School Heads, especially those of the larger schools, have more in common with other members of the Head Masters' Conference than with other Secondary School Heads.[1]

---

[1] The organisation, aims and work of the Head Masters' Conference are outlined in the *Public Schools' Year Book* and in Truman and Knightley's " *Schools* " both to be found in any good reference library, and re-issued annually.

Briefly, it is a Head Masters' Club, meeting annually in full Conference at Oxford, Cambridge or some other University town (Durham was chosen in 1961) and electing, on a mainly regional basis, a Committee which meets six times a year. There are 200 full members in the British Isles, some 30-40 overseas, and a few Associate Members (retired Headmasters and former Headmasters now doing other work as bishops, University principals etc.).

Any school whose Head Master is a member of the H.M.C. is automatically regarded as a Public School and as such entitled to use the services of the Public Schools Appointments Board and enter its boys for sporting events reserved to Public School boys (e.g. certain skiing races). Representation on the Governing Bodies' Association also confers Public School status: a few schools belong to the G.B.A. but not the H.M.C., having lost their place in the latter because they are co-educational (Dollar, Bedales, St. George's Harpenden) or too small to support a Sixth Form of adequate size. The main criteria for admission are:

    (i)   Independent or Grant-Aided status (a few other well-established schools have been allowed to *remain* members);

    (ii) Absence of girls;

The Independent Schools are of much the same type as
in England, except that there are very few (if any) of the
somewhat dubious kind found especially south of the Thames.
If a Scottish parent is not satisfied with the national system he
will not have anything less than an H.M.C. boarding school or
the equivalent type of girls' school preceded—though not always
—by a good preparatory school. He does not see any virtue in
mere "independence" without definite *educational* advantages
attached, nor does he regard an acquired or artificially maintained accent as a substitute for sound learning. If an
independent school cannot give better academic results than the

---

    (iii) Number of boys in the Sixth Form or doing Sixth Form work;
    (iv) Number of old boys at Universities;
    (v) General reputation and tone of the School.

Members of the Conference discuss education, administration and any
other relevant business, but the Conference as a whole does not take
decisions binding on its members as individual Headmasters.

In principle there is no such thing as a " greater " or a " lesser "
Public School and all members are regarded as equal by virtue of their
membership. On the other hand there are certain schools whose Headmaster is automatically elected to the Conference and others whose position
is reconsidered whenever there is a new Head.

The following Scottish Schools are represented on the Head Masters'
Conference: Fettes, Glasgow Academy, Glenalmond, Gordonstoun, Loretto,
Merchiston Castle, Strathallan, Edinburgh Academy (all Independent),
Daniel Stewart's, George Heriot's and George Watson's of Edinburgh and
Robert Gordon's of Aberdeen (Grant-Aided). In addition Dollar Academy
is represented on the Governing Bodies' Association as are all the above
except Robert Gordon's.

All Head Masters' Conference Schools are briefly described in the
Public Schools' Year Book, as are—still more briefly, those preparatory
schools represented in the Incorporated Association of Preparatory Schools,
a similar but larger body.

Qualifications for membership of the I.A.P.S. are

(a) *Independent status*, and recognition by the Ministry of Education
in England or the Scottish Education Department here. English preparatory schools are not eligible for membership unless recognised as
" efficient " but may function if " registered " as tolerable. In Scotland
there is no distinction made between registration and recognition.

(b) *Predominance of boys* (there may be a few girls, especially
masters' daughters) and *absence of boys over the age of 15.* Headmistresses
are not eligible but a school may be conducted by a Headmaster's widow
and her son, not yet experienced enough to take full responsibility—and
he will be eligible for membership if academically qualified and in other
respects acceptable.

(c) *General reputation* (schools aspiring to membership are dis-
creetly investigated and are visited by one or more I.A.P.S. Heads).

H.M.C. and I.A.P.S. schools, even in Scotland, are very largely staffed
by graduates of Oxford and Cambridge. A strong leavening of " Oxbridge "
graduates might be desirable in many of our Secondary Schools. Perhaps
it will come now that Scottish students are eligible for grants to attend
universities furth of Scotland, the regulations which prevented this having
been rescinded early in 1961.

nearest "State" establishment, it is not worth the waste of money.

The *minimum standard* of independent education is therefore much higher than that of public education as a whole and the *average* corresponds approximately to that of the grant-aided schools with perhaps fewer university places won but other advantages to compensate.

The *maximum standard* reached by these schools is not as high as the best English schools of the same type, but Eton and Winchester for instance are older, wealthier and more firmly rooted than any boarding school in Scotland. They are also much larger. Some English schools, furthermore, have a fair number of Scottish boys, mainly belonging to the aristocracy and landed gentry, and the absence of these boys prevents the Scottish schools from reaching the same level of "social desirability", although they are good of their kind and fully comparable with English schools of the same size (200-400 boys) and age (80-110 years old). Indeed they may be better because in England there is an ascending (or descending) scale of social eligibility among "Public Schools", causing many Old Boys of minor public schools to send their sons to schools in the "first twenty" and these again to send their sons to Eton if possible and otherwise to Harrow or one of three or four others. This scale does not operate in Scotland except in so far as a very few English Public Schools may be thought (by some) superior to any of ours.

As in England the boys' schools generally divide into preparatory schools with a 7-13 or 8-13 range and Public Schools with a 13-18 range. The girls' schools follow a similar pattern but the "transfer age" is 11 or 12. There are a few minor aberrations. Thus Blanerne, basically a preparatory school, retains some less able boys beyond the age of 13; Fort Augustus has a primary school intake at 12 and a preparatory school intake at 13.

Academically the preparatory schools differ from primary schools in that class teachers do not operate beyond the first or second year. Thereafter specialists or semi-specialists take over and languages appear on the curriculum as in a senior secondary school.

At various ages preparatory school boys will therefore be ahead of primary school pupils of equivalent ability in some subjects and behind in others. Thus at 9 they may be slightly ahead all round. At 11 they will be well ahead in languages and history, slightly behind in English, well behind in Arithmetic. At 13 they will have made up the leeway in English and Arithmetic but lost some of their lead in languages, the pace at this stage being slower than in S.I and S.II. After a year at their Public School they will be ahead all round once more, mainly because it is at this age that day school pupils are most vulnerable to the many possible distractions inherent in their way of life, and that a good Housemaster, having dealt with the problems of puberty in a hundred cases and more over the past few years, may prove vastly more competent than the average parent.

As between " Public " and Senior Secondary Schools, the former, *quâ* schools, have nearly all the advantages, beside the essential one of not having to take anybody they don't want. Their boys arrive with the change-over to subject teaching and to a secondary curriculum well behind them—it is only to the change of social climate and to being juniors once more that they need adapt themselves. *Common Entrance* is in itself a more satisfactory examination than the " Qualifying " in that it covers the whole range of the subjects they have been taught, while the questions are so framed that they " extend " the boy further in the subjects common to both examinations. The way of life is more conducive to disciplined and persistent effort. Last but not least there are *more* masters, and they are generally thought to be *better* both as teachers and still more as all-round educators.

One very important point is that masters and mistresses in fee-paying schools have a sense of *personal obligation* towards their pupils and the parents of those pupils. It is not merely a question of educating these pupils " according to their aptitude " but of achieving a definite target, and increasing their aptitude in order to achieve it, if need be.

The question of whether my preparatory school or Millfield pupils ought to be got through their exams never occurred to me when I was in the independent system. If they had less than what, in the " State " system, would be regarded as the I.Q. required to place them in the academic stream, I simply put in that much more effort to get them through in my subjects. Nearly all of my colleagues had the same outlook, which was expected of us—we were not prepared to accept failure for our pupils or for ourselves.

In the " State " system the prevailing attitude seems to be that one takes one's pupils as they are—if they have it in them to pass examinations, so much the better; if not, why worry? There are more than enough able pupils to fill the universities, and does it really matter whether this one gets in rather than that one? It may to him, but not to the community at large.

The " State " school teacher's loyalty, where it intervenes, is to the community as a whole. This may be a nobler emotion than personal loyalty to known individuals, but it is generally a less potent motive, and I think there may be a slightly greater tendency to regard teaching as just " a job ", which one does conscientiously and well but without any personal involvement.

From this flow various consequences.

(1) The switch from system to system is not readily made. Those who come to Independent schools with a " State-bred " outlook are in many cases a failure because, although classes are smaller and teaching techniques less important, more " self-giving " is required and they may not have the right sort of " self " to give.

Those who cross in the reverse direction, as I have done, also fail to adjust their approach. They cannot acquire the impersonal attitude expected from servants of the public, even in the modified and humanised form which is regarded as suitable for teachers.

A number of pupils do not take to the sort of outlook which I have so far retained. Others may take to it very readily, and the result is that performance, within any given class, becomes much more strung out than if that same class were taken by a teacher with the more usual outlook. This may in turn set up a mild " chain reaction " in other subjects.

(2) Other things being equal, or even moderately weighted in favour of the " State " school (which may, for instance, have more up-to-date buildings and equipment and better-qualified teachers) the independent school will probably achieve more with any given pupil, because he will not be allowed to drift—and " finding one's own level " is often little more than drifting.

(3) Independent schools can make good use at all levels of a very wide assortment of men whose knowledge and enthusiasm make up for that lack of technique. They include late entrants to the profession, as well as men who have taught then gone into, some other career, and returned to teaching in their 'fifties or exceptionally their sixties. It is partly for this

*THE COOKERY LESSON AT
KIRKCALDY HIGH SCHOOL.*

ON A SAILING COURSE AT RANNOCH SCHOOL

MAINTENANCE OF FIRE BRIGADE PUMP
AT RANNOCH SCHOOL

reason that their staffing problems are less severe than those of
"State" schools generally.

(4) The work and the life are more satisfying in themselves
and leave less time and energy for all manner of bitterness and
recrimination. Certain conferences, which shall be nameless and
occur mainly south of the Border, have perennial resolutions
calling for the abolition of independent schools, of selective
schools and even of streaming within schools. But I have never
heard of the Head Masters' Conference or of the Incorporated
Association of Assistant Masters demanding that fees be charged
in all grammar schools, or that independent schools should
receive subsidies while retaining their independence, or that
comprehensive schools should be abolished. They are quite
content to meet old friends, consume a reasonable amount of
sherry and discuss their own problems.

I must add that the very great majority of "State" school
teachers are neither vindictive nor militant except where they
feel they have had a raw deal. Nevertheless the conditions
under which they work give more scope to a noisy minority who
attract more attention than many of us, in both systems, think
they deserve.

The position on the Continent and in Scandinavia is somewhat different, at least in the Senior Secondary schools. These
very often charge fees, nominal enough but fees nevertheless,
perhaps in the region of £3 to £5 a term. The postponement
of earning capacity and the lack of maintenance grants, together
with the character of the entrance examination or other selection
procedure (I.Q.'s are never used) make them into largely upper
middle-class or middle-class preserves, very similar in outlook
to our grant-aided schools, and quite unlike the public secondary
schools of towns where grant-aided schools also flourish. The
personal motive comes in to a considerable extent, especially
near the top (most of the working-class pupils have by then
dropped out) and one finds professional men mainly engaged
in teaching the sons of other professional men, plus a minority
who have been effectively absorbed into the Sixth Form network
of friendships, interests and preoccupations.

It is in this personal link between master and pupil that
the strength of independent schools very largely resides. The
link also exists in public secondary schools but incidentally
rather than as their dominant feature. Before the advent of
secondary education for all it was certainly much closer,

especially between the village dominie and the lad o' pairts, who provided the dominie's main reason for taking on a job that never was materially very rewarding and has always involved a good deal of drudgery if properly done.

It is in some ways a dangerous link—not morally but through its inevitable exclusiveness. The night is darkest as seen from a well-lit room and coldest when one is just out of range of a fire, seen and envied but too remote to give of its warmth.

On the other hand a well-balanced staff can and *should* contain teachers who, *between them,* will make some sort of impact in nearly every pupil in the school. More regard should be paid to this and less to the respective claims of " Chapter V " and " Article 39 ".

What is harder to establish is whether the combination of home, local and school life as experienced by the day school pupil is more or less educative than that of home life for a shorter period and school life for a longer one. The boarding school pupil must largely do without local life, since he is never in his home locality long enough to take an active part in whatever is going on there—while at school he is more or less completely isolated from what goes on beyond the gates.

There is no way, as I see it, to arrive at a definite and objective answer: so much depends on the boy, his home, his school and his locality; what he has may be more or less worth having; what he misses may be a great or a trivial loss. Much also depends on what one regards as most important in his total experience of life. A view commonly held—in theory at least—is that boys gain on balance from being sent to a boarding school while girls lose; but there are now as many girls in these schools as there are boys.

A more important question is whether the existence of grant-aided and independent schools is beneficial to Scottish Education and to Scotland as a country, admitting—as most people who have thought seriously and dispassionately on the problem admit—that they probably do better for their few pupils than " ordinary schools " for the many who attend them.

One may start from the assumption that the best has a natural right to exist and that by existing it sets an absolute standard. This, roughly, was Plato's viewpoint and I make no bones about acknowledging that—emotionally at least—it is also mine. But emotion ought to have no place in a discussion of this kind, even though many people unconsciously allow it to slide in by one of many little back doors.

Or one may try to balance the greater good of a smaller number against the smaller good of a greater number. How far do ordinary day schools suffer from the absence of their potential first 3% (taking all secondary schools) or their potential 10% (taking *academic* streams and schools only) or their potential first 30% (taking the *upper forms* of these streams and schools only)?

The only way is to compare (a) the public Senior Secondary schools of towns where they hold the field alone, with no possible competition except from boarding schools at some considerable distance, with those of (b) towns with no fee-paying school, but within the possible outer catchment area of Edinburgh, (c) towns with such a school and (d) Edinburgh, where fee-paying schools predominate at that academic level.

Inverness is a fair example of (a), Galashiels; of (b), Aberdeen and Dundee of (c). I would have to know far more about these towns and their schools to make the comparison myself—except to say that in Edinburgh, precisely because everybody has heard of the fee-paying schools, both independent and grant-aided, nobody has heard of the rest unless he was educated there himself.[1] But Edinburgh is a unique case, not only in Scotland but in North-Western Europe as a whole. I cannot think of any city of comparable size with so many independent or semi-independent schools of good repute.

Another possible comparison is with other European countries where Independent Secondary Schools are either considerably more or considerably less prevalent than here. Sweden has four, Finland over a hundred, Norway and Denmark one each. In Holland they are in overwhelming majority: in France they have about 40% of the secondary school population.

Firstly to dispose of Finland. There it is purely the luck of the draw whether your school happens to be State-run, municipal or independent but grant-aided. There is no social significance attached, except that the "Swedes" tend to frequent their own independent schools and it is slightly more "U" to speak Swedish. At least the Swedish-speakers think so.

---

[1] This may be a slight exaggeration: Boroughmuir has built up a solid reputation for Modern Languages and Rugger. Nevertheless anybody who thinks of "Edinburgh schools" will probably think of the fee-paying schools first.

In Sweden, Denmark and Norway the independent schools are too few to make a great deal of difference. The general tendency is for those who get into an academic secondary school to stay at least until they are 17 and have taken Real-Examen (approximately our new "O" grade or the English "O" level, but with a slightly lower passmark and a necessity to pass in a set range of subjects). But the proportion of pupils with an upper middle-class background is decidedly higher especially at the top of the gymnasia, and "working-class" pupils are only about half as likely to reach the Universities as they are here. The four Swedish boarding schools are commonly supposed to have a lower academic standard but a more desirable social atmosphere than many gymnasia. The Danish one, Sorø Academy, enjoys high prestige both academically and socially.

In Holland it is essentially a matter of religion. Catholics and active Protestants run their own schools, fully subsidized by the State and conducted in accordance with the Dutch equivalent of our Schools Code. "Humanists" use the 'State' Schools.[1] Whether or not one or the other communities' schools has a better academic reputation you still send your children to the school belonging to your own "pillar". Everything is organized in this way, even football clubs, stamp collecting and radio networks.

In France again it is largely a matter of religion, though many who are not practising Catholics will send their sons to a Catholic College on the principle that faith is a standby in adolescence. The boys will lapse when they grow up but will again send *their* sons to a College on the same principle. It is widely believed that the *lycées* (State) are academically superior but that the Colleges give a better all-round education and maintain a more satisfactory atmosphere.

My view, based mainly on experience of Scandinavia and of Holland where Catholic and Protestant schools, though technically independent, fall into the same range of academic categories and social types as state schools, and are fully maintained out of public funds, is that if we had "state" schools in complete or almost complete possession of the field, the following developments would occur:

(1) The proportion of those staying on beyond the minimum leaving age would greatly increase, and that of pupils lasting out the Highers course would double. In particular,

[1] These are, in fact, municipal.

early leaving would entirely disappear among pupils with a middle-class background, however marginal.

(2) The proportion of senior secondary pupils with a middle class background would increase, due to entry into the academic stream becoming more competitive than at present, and to these pupils being better placed both to get in and stay in.

(3) In consequence the "streams" and schools (where Senior Secondary schools pure and simple existed) would become more sharply divided along class lines, and friendships between pupils of different streams, schools or social backgrounds would become rarer. This is the case in Sweden, where everybody mixes in the folkskola (primary school) and to a lesser extent in the *realskola*, but where those who survive to enter the *gymnasium* proper (S.IV upwards) soon lose sight of their former comrades.

(4) Working-class pupils surviving thus far would be rapidly absorbed into the middle class, and would buy integration within the school at the price of becoming strangers in their own homes.

(5) The final outcome would be less democracy rather than more, though class divisions might not follow quite the same lines as at present. On the other hand it is probable that average academic standards would be raised all round and that the pool of ability would be tapped more effectively than at present. Whether, in order to achieve this, it is worth while arriving at a situation wherein nearly all members of the middle class are demonstrably brighter than nearly all members of the working class (and this is more or less true of Sweden and of Holland) is another matter. Personally I don't like the idea and feel it goes against the Scottish grain.

On this ground alone I would oppose, and most strongly, any attempt to interfere with the Grant-Aided Schools which are unquestionably Scottish in their aims (*academic* rather than "character" education), their curriculum, and their final product. What of the Independent Schools?

Again no one seriously disputes their academic efficiency and they are commonly supposed to give a better education all-round than all except a few of the very best Senior Secondary schools. Nor is it denied that they can do a better job for the "marginal type of boy" who would just have scraped through into a one-language stream in the "State" system, or just failed to make it, but who at all events would have been a very doubtful Certificate candidate. A preparatory school, with classes averaging 10-15 pupils, will get him through Common Entrance at 13, because it is expected to do so and that is what his parents are paying for. A primary school with classes of 35-40 is under no such obligation to get any one individual through "Qualifying" at 12. Subsequently this same boy will almost certainly take half a dozen "O" levels and may even, if a "late developer", manage a couple of "A's". In the State system he would be carried along with the "technical" stream or struggle with the tail of the "language pupils"—in either case leaving at 15 or possibly 16.

The accusations most frequently made against these schools are precisely that (1) they load the dice against rather brighter but not outstanding pupils from the public secondary schools and—to a lesser extent—from the grant-aided schools, since it takes less ability to complete the academic course in a boarding school than in a day school and especially in a day school with a proportion of non-academic pupils, and (2) they are, educationally speaking, foreign enclaves—a kind of scholastic Gibraltar or Guantanamo.[1]

On the first count I think there is no real answer. The Public and Preparatory schools between them tap the pool of ability—within the small section of the population that uses them—very thoroughly indeed, and they deserve credit for so doing. If the same were to be done for all Scottish children and adolescents by the "State" system, annual expenditure on education by taxpayers and—in so far as fees were charged—by parents would run to an average of at least £300 on each of 800,000 pupils aged 8-17, in order to provide them with boarding accommodation and reduce classes to 20 pupils or under) plus £75 on each of 200,000 aged 5-8. In fact it would probably come to more because "State" schools are built on a more lavish scale than the older independent schools. Scotland would not get away with much less than £300,000,000, and for Britain as a whole the figure would approach £3,000,000,000 before one had even started to think about higher education in all its varied and expensive forms. At the moment Britain spends under £1,000,000,000 on *all* education.

But in that event either University entrance would have to become even more competitive than at present, with the bulk

[1] The American base in Cuba.

of potential students deflected — as in Russia — to "parallel establishments" or we should face a grave problem of graduate unemployment, as Greece does, with a severe shortage of people willing to take on the rough and unintellectual jobs which have to be done if civilized society is to be kept going. A very competitive entry—anything much more competitive than at present—would transform and I think ruin the character of our Universities and in particular of St. Andrews. They would lose the steady intake of good but not outstanding students who make their mark in extra-curricular societies and informal groups of friends rather than in the examination room, but whose contribution to the life of the community is none the less valuable for that.

If one accepts that it is not only impossible but even undesirable to give every pupil the opportunities given to fairly dull ones within the independent system one must then ask whether it is right that young people who have money behind them should be able to obtain the necessary paper qualifications with far less effort than the rest. Are the qualifications, under such conditions, even equivalent? Do three " A's " and three " O's " or four " Highers " and two " Lowers ", represent the same amount of ability, effort and determination if taken by a boy in a boarding school with classes of 10-20 as if they had been taken by a pupil in a mixed day school with classes of 25-30 or more? I think not.

The answer would not be, however, to abolish the independent schools but to demand a higher standard from those who attend them, and it seems employers are beginning to do this. The bureau which specializes in placing Public School boys *without degrees* in suitable jobs has achieved, of late, only moderate success—at any rate in its Northern branch. Even "father's firm" is more and more inclined to expect a degree.

On the second count the charge, *for what it is worth*, is partly proved. Schools such as Glenalmond, Fettes and Gordonstoun are not, strictly speaking, in the Scottish educational tradition. Most of them try to do a job which Scottish parents do not normally expect from Scottish schools. Their basic aims, curriculum and examinations are English: so are in most cases the Universities which the boys hope to enter. But most of the boys are Scottish and they are at least being educated in their own country. If these schools did not exist the boys would in some cases be sent to Senior Secondary Schools instead, but most of them would go furth of Scotland. In any case, what is the charge worth?

Merely because the ideals followed by these schools are English it does not automatically mean they are *worse*. It is perhaps the Scottish principle of a clearcut division of labour between home and community on one side and school on the other, that is out of date in a modern industrial society. It is at least arguable that the English scheme of examinations is in itself sounder provided that excessive specialization can somehow be avoided. A strong case can be made out for transfer at 13 rather than 12 but coupled with the introduction of languages, algebra, geometry and specialist teaching in the upper reaches of the primary department.

Intellectual isolationism is, ultimately, the death of intellect itself. The English-type schools are valuable largely because they are different and provide at the same time a point of comparison for the questing and an alternative for the dissatisfied.

In any case our forthcoming entry into the Common Market and the increasing unification of Europe will lay Scotland open to many other influences, some of which may help to cancel out the English. An attitude of distrust and latent hostility towards all things Southern served a purpose earlier on, as a means to keep the nation in being. There is far less justification for it now.

Another point is that the typically Scottish schools, whatever their other merits, have done little to foster any sense of loyalty to Scotland, or of pride in her distinctive achievements in the past. I have already mentioned this in discussing the History curriculum. It would be an interesting exercise in social research to take a cross-section of Sixth Forms at the Scottish " Public", Grant-Aided and Senior Secondary Schools over a period extending say from 1950 to 1960 and consider what has become of the boys in these forms. What sort of jobs have they taken, and where? How many have remained in Scotland? Of those who have gone to England or further afield, how many first tried to find something in their own country? Of those who have stayed, how many have done so because there happened to be something going that suited them, and how many as a matter of deliberate choice, because they preferred life in Scotland or felt under some sort of moral obligation towards her?

I have a feeling that one would find a surprisingly high proportion of young men with an "English" education still here and a surprisingly high proportion of those with a "Scottish" one away. But the facts and the motives alike deserve a closer look. Until they come out, whose prerogative is it to cast the first stone at the English-type schools?

The positive case for the defence, as distinct from mere whittling away of the arguments commonly used against these schools, is stronger than their opponents like to believe. It rests essentially on their value as an example of what *can* be done.

Some people will say there is no fair comparison because of the natural advantages which boarding schools, as such, enjoy. But one merit of these schools is precisely that they compel the fair-minded critic and the educational reformer to consider whether there might not be a greater place for boarding schools within the "state" system, either as fully-fledged secondary schools, or possibly taking boys from industrial areas for the last year of the junior secondary course, and doing things with them that cannot be done in their present school and home surroundings. (See also Chapter VIII.)

Apart from the advantages which they enjoy as *boarding* schools, there are others attaching to them as *independent* schools. In the first place the Headmaster has, in general, much greater freedom of action and it is easier for him, in the circumstances, to give of his best. In the "State" system too much depends on the outlook of the local authority—some, e.g. Fife, being considerably better than others in this respect. This greater freedom of action means that the Headmaster has fewer administrative duties since besides running the school which is his proper job, he is not obliged to give such a detailed and continuous account of his stewardship. He therefore finds more time to teach, and this is obviously a good thing, because there is no equally effective way to know what is going on in the school and because Headmasters are supposed to be and probably are the ablest and most distinguished men in the profession.

Secondly, as part of this greater freedom of action, the Headmaster appoints his own staff. He chooses his men for their ability to do the job and to fit in the existing community both of masters alone and of masters and boys. In general he requires a good degree and, from the younger men, some measure of athletic powers, or at any rate willingness to pull their sporting weight. He is not interested in the training college diploma or Dip. Ed., which is not really relevant to this kind of work, with smaller classes and more easily-controlled pupils than in most day schools. " Non-educational " considerations, such as may intervene in some local authority schools, especially where senior appointments are concerned, generally play no part whatever, except that a Catholic Headmaster will first look for a *suitably qualified* co-religionist, failing which he will take a Protestant with a good degree rather than a Catholic with an indifferent one.

Arising from the manner of his appointment, an Independent school master is in a stronger and more satisfactory position than a secondary school teacher. He is dealing all the time with a more qualified colleague—namely his Headmaster—not with an educational civil servant, a non-teaching Head and ultimately a committee of amateurs, who control education on the principle that the expert should be on tap, not on top, and that common sense matters more than specialist knowledge. The Governors almost certainly know far more about their particular school, and about education generally, than an Education Committee can be expected to know about any one school or the work it does, and yet they almost certainly interfere less.

Again, the master in an Independent School is employed in a more distinctive and distinguished capacity than the cooks, gardeners, etc., who are ancillary to the school community, not part of it in the same sense that he is. They are servants, if no longer described as such, and come under the Bursar: he is a master and his only superior is the Head. " Teachers " lack this definite professional status — indeed they have lost what there was of it, with the loss of their older title and the appearance of a vast host of ancillary personnel all on the same county pay-roll.

Another feature of his greater independence, within a school itself more independent, is that he can order textbooks when he wants them—within reasonable limits—instead of having to wait for requisition time, and the same goes for the less expensive items of equipment.

I am convinced that educational standards in the public secondary schools would rise and rise quickly if these could somehow be made to approximate more closely to the Independent schools as regards the freedom and status of their Heads and staff. *Even at present salary scales* (and the Independent schools pay only a little more, with a much longer incremental period) they would find their staffing problems diminished and their morale raised all round.

One could then consider the case for higher salaries coupled with a substantial lengthening of the school day. This would make it possible to have afternoon classes from 4 till 6 instead of 1-15 till 4, with the first afternoon period transferred to the morning, and games and other activities filling in the early afternoon as in boarding schools.

It might also be possible to transfer some of the existing load of homework into the normal school day, remembering that forty minutes of it done in school under supervision are probably worth over an hour at home and one is at least certain that the work is done!

The sense of community, not only among the boys but *between masters and boys* is another essential element in the strength of the Independent Schools. It arises largely from belonging to the same small minority and is therefore strongest at Eton and Harrow, and the Catholic Schools, which educate minorities within the minority. It cannot therefore exist to quite the same extent within day schools, but there is certainly room for more of it. The main practical effects are felt at and near the top. The masters take a greater interest in the boys, even if they are not particularly bright, and are more inclined to do all they can to help them on, even though it involves a considerable sacrifice of leisure and home life in term time, for which they make up by having longer holidays (eight or nine weeks in summer, four or five at Christmas and again at Easter). At the same time senior boys must show a greater sense of responsibility and a greater willingness to co-operate not only with the Head but with all masters and especially their Housemaster.

The House system itself could be made far more realistic than it is at present in most of those day schools which have it. Here again it is to the Independent Schools that we must turn for an example. They, of course, have greater opportunities for making it work, but even in a day school much can be done if one has a mind to do it. The first thing is to reduce the size of Houses to about sixty pupils each. The second is to increase the number of activities in which the House engages as a house and of occasions on which it meets—also to provide it with some meeting place other than a classroom. Thirdly teachers not in charge of a House should not only be attached to one in name, but entrusted with definite duties therein, as are House Tutors (assistant House Masters) in those boarding schools which have them.

There is far more that could be said on the subject, in a larger book, but I hope this is enough to show that ignorant hostility towards the Independent Schools, based on refusal to ascertain the facts, is not worthy of those who are under the impression that they think.

Finally there is the small matter of parents' rights. So far as I can judge the Independent Schools certainly give the best education to those who can afford their fees. In doing so they reduce the opportunities available not to the brightest but to the fairly bright among the great majority educated in the " State " system. Their " anti-Scottish " influence has probably been exaggerated while the " pro-Scottish" influence of the day schools is very much in doubt. They save the state the not inconsiderable expense of providing for the education of some 17,000 children and adolescents, whose parents nevertheless help to pay for the education of the other 880,000.

On balance and from a public rather than a private stand-point there may—depending on one's ultimate values—be slightly more to be said against them than for them, but only to the extent that, *if one were starting again from scratch* one might prefer to be without them and educate all the nation's children in the nation's own schools. But we are not starting again from scratch. The Independent Schools exist and do a very fine job in their rather narrow sector (2% of all Scottish Education). The parents like them and are prepared to pay. We cannot deny them the right to do as they will with their own.

A left-wing schoolmaster, who saw the rough draft of my book, took strong exception to this last sentence, his opinion being that, " the whole of modern government depends on depriving people of the right to do what they like with their own."

I do not fully accept the philosophical basis of " modern government "—nor, fortunately, do all those who are involved in administration, education or the forming of public opinion.

Certain restraints must be placed on individual liberty, but these should be as few as possible and should be regarded as lesser evils tolerated in the over-riding public interest, rather than as normal and healthy.

Two principles are at stake—the right of *citizens* to spend their own money (what is left of it after taxation) and the right of *parents* to bring up their own children as they see fit, so long as they observe the basic decencies.

There is also the practical point that nobody can prevent parents from spending money on the education of their children. If it is not on school fees it will be on something else, cultural rather than curricular. The experience of Switzerland, Germany and several other countries proves this quite conclusively.

CHAPTER VI

The Colleges of Education

Scottish teachers, if men or if in secondary schools, are
required to take a university degree or its equivalent *and* undergo
a course of training (normally lasting a year) in a College of
Education. Their English colleagues qualify on the degree or
training alone, and these two qualifications are supposedly inter-
changeable. In practice things do not quite work out that way.
English primary schools will take a trained non-graduate in
preference to an untrained graduate, and indeed in preference
to a trained graduate, who is more expensive to employ. English
grammar schools are more interested in the degree, though post-
graduate training gives added security, a small but useful
increment, and preference where the appointing authority is in
the fortunate position of being able to choose between candidates
with equally good degrees. Interchangeability only operates in
secondary modern and comprehensive schools.

There are several other differences between English and
Scottish qualifications. Thus any degree, in England, is *ipso
facto* a teaching qualification (and any good honours degree is
a good qualification). English is often taught by men with Classics
or History degrees; with a degree in a " non-teaching " subject
(e.g. Moral Philosophy or Economics) an Englishman may very
well teach languages or Mathematics in his own country. In
Scotland, however, a graduate is only qualified to teach those
subjects which he has studied at University. This leads to what
an Englishman would regard as flagrant anomalies. Thus an
Honours Classicist or historian may very well happen to have
near-bilingual fluency in French and/or German. In an emergency he may be called upon to teach those subjects in addition
to or even instead of his own and he may make a very good job

of it. But he can be replaced at any time by an ordinary graduate whose degree happens to have included languages at a much lower level of effective performance.

The reason is that, in Scotland, any teacher with the appropriate qualifications has an established right to displace any teacher without these qualifications. Thus:

(1) A certificated teacher of French has a right to replace an uncertificated teacher who happens to be teaching French. But he could not, unless also qualified in mathematics, replace an uncertificated mathematician.

(2) A certificated teacher of Classics has a right to replace a certificated teacher of English or History who happens to be teaching Classics.

(3) In those posts which require an honours degree, the holder of such a degree, even if his teaching ability is only just adequate, has a right to replace even an outstanding teacher with an ordinary degree in the same subject.

This does not apply in England, where there is no established right to be employed in any capacity. A Headmaster or Education Committee might replace a teacher in the circumstances above, but would be under no obligation to do so. In the first case they might easily decide that the uncertificated teacher knew more French; in the second they might consider that the historian was also a useful cricket coach: in the third they would almost certainly prefer to leave well alone.

On the other hand a teacher who is dismissed has in general no redress in England, unless he is employed under contract for a definite period of time. He is entitled to a term's notice or a term's salary in lieu of notice, but has no right to be reinstated. If an Education Committee in England decided it was against public policy to employ red-haired men, or hook-nosed women, the persons thus dismissed—so long as they had adequate notice —could do nothing about it.

Graduates in England are usually trained in University Departments of Education, if they elect to train. Many do not, because their degree itself confers the status of a qualified teacher, which they lose if they attempt but fail to complete a course of training. Scottish graduates, however, are trained in Colleges of Education, whether they have taken an ordinary degree or an honours degree. Most of these colleges also provide courses for non-graduate women and for teachers of technical subjects, who have previously taken a qualification regarded as being in some sense the equivalent of a degree (together with the training course it entitles them to teach their subject or subjects in a secondary school, but does not confer graduate status upon them).

The English Dip.Ed., is a teaching qualification, useful though not essential. The Scottish Dip.Ed., is mainly a *personal* qualification, though it gives its holders exemption from College of Education courses in education and psychology. It is also a useful added qualification for those who later wish to transfer to educational administration, but it is not an essential prerequisite of such a career.

The Scottish Dip.Ed. and teacher training course, however, are often taken concurrently and many set or recommended books are common to both. The Colleges of Education are all in the cities and therefore close to one or the other of the Scottish Universities.

Three different types of authority may run training establishments in England. Most teacher training colleges (for non-graduates) belong to local authorities. A smaller number belong to voluntary bodies—mainly the Church of England and the Catholic Church. Departments of Education are fully under the control of the Universities: local authorities and religious bodies only have such influence over them as may derive from their representation on the University Court in the " Redbricks ", and none at all at Oxford and Cambridge, which are entirely autonomous.

All the Scottish Colleges of Education, however, are administered in the same way. Each has a Governing Body, with 25 members at Moray House (Edinburgh) and Jordanhill (Glasgow), 24 at Dundee and Aberdeen, 17 at Craiglockhart (R.C. women, Edinburgh) and Notre Dame (R.C. women, Glasgow) and 16 at Dunfermline College, Aberdeen (Physical Education, women).

The four main colleges train (a) Graduate men, irrespective of religion; (b) non-Catholic women, with or without degrees; (c) teachers of technical subjects. They recruit mainly but not exclusively on a regional basis; i.e. candidates from the south-east of Scotland normally train at Moray House, those from the south-west and west, at Jordanhill, those from the east at Dundee, those from the north at Aberdeen. This regional recruitment is reflected in the composition of their governing bodies. Each includes Education Committee members and teachers in various categories

(Senior Secondary, Junior Secondary and Primary Heads, the principal of a central institution or head teacher of a further education centre, and two others) from its own area. There are also, in each case, three representatives of the adjacent university.

The Education Committee members are appointed

(a) by the Education authority of the city in which the college is situated;

(b) by the Association of County Councils in Scotland.

The University representatives are appointed by the Senate of the University.

The teachers' representatives are elected by certificated teachers, within the area. Thus all certificated teachers in the South-East vote for three head teachers, one further education principal or head teacher and two other teachers, irrespective of the post in which they are employed (as a rule they are not Heads, but can be) to serve as Governors of Moray House.

In addition there are two representatives of the Church of Scotland, appointed by the educational committee of its General Assembly, and three Governors appointed by the Secretary of State, who may but need not be "educationists". The Secretary of State may appoint two Assessors: the University Senate and the Association of Directors of Education may, on a regional basis as above, appoint one assessor each. These assessors may attend and speak at meetings of the Governing Bodies and their committees and sub-committees, but have no vote.

The Governing Body of Moray House appoints a representative to serve on the Governing Body of Craiglockhart, and vice versa. A similar arrangement exists in Glasgow, between Jordanhill and Notre Dame, and this is the reason why the Moray House and Jordanhill Governing Bodies are larger than those at Aberdeen and Dundee.

The two Catholic colleges are not directly administered by the Church as diocesan training colleges are in England. Their Governing Bodies have five Local Authority representatives instead of eight, one university representative instead of three and two nominees of the Secretary of State instead of three. There are four teachers' representatives instead of six. Three are appointed by the Guild of Catholic Teachers, one by the Educational Institute of Scotland. These two bodies and the S.S.A.[1]

---

[1] Scottish Schoolmasters' Association. Only men not being members of the E.I.S. are eligible to this body.

and S.S.T.A.[2] have no direct say in the election of teachers to the Governing Bodies of the four main colleges—they can only advise their members to vote for certain candidates.

The Catholic Church is represented, as such, by two nominees of the Hierarchy and by the Sister Superior of the Convent to which the college land and buildings belong.

The Episcopalian Church was formerly represented, as such, on the Training Authority at Aberdeen. It has lost its sole official representative. But many if not most of the " county class " are Episcopalians and their Church is therefore indirectly represented through the Education Committee members.

The two Catholic Colleges are "regional" to the extent that Notre Dame has Education Authority representaives from Glasgow and the South-Western area (including Argyllshire) while Craiglockhart has them from Edinburgh and the rest of Scotland. No such regulation applies to the teachers' representatives, however, since Catholic teachers from the north of Scotland (which includes quite large areas with a mainly Catholic population) train at either college indifferently.

The College of Physical Education has one representative each of Aberdeen City education authority and Aberdeen University. Its other Governors are non-regional and only one need be a serving teacher, appointed by the E.I.S.

The seven Governing Bodies each have much the same powers and responsibilities as a County Education Committee has, with regard to the schools in its area. These powers and responsibilities are set out in the Teachers (Training Authorities) (Scotland) Regulations, 1958. Colleges of Education are financed by local authorities and by the Scottish Education Department to the extent of 40% and 60% respectively, more or less.

The work of the seven Governing Bodies is co-ordinated by the Scottish Council for the Training of Teachers, which has other functions of its own set out in the regulations quoted above [recognition of teachers trained outwith Scotland, inspection of the Governing Bodies' annual estimates, etc.]

---

[2] Scottish Secondary Teachers' Association. Only graduates or "equivalent persons" teaching in secondary schools or the secondary departments of primary-secondary schools, are eligible to this body. They must not belong to the E.I.S.

The E.I.S. (Educational Institute of Scotland) admits both men and women, graduates and non-graduates, so long as they are certificated teachers. It has a large majority of non-graduate women, but also includes more graduates, and more men, than either the S.S.A. or the S.S.T.A.

The Scottish Council consists mainly of members of the Seven Governing Bodies mentioned above. The seven chairmen sit *ex officio*. The Governing Bodies between them nominate 21 other persons (Jordanhill 5, Moray House 4, Aberdeen and Dundee, 3 each, other colleges 2 each). Out of these the Secretary of State appoints 13 to 16 members. These and the seven chairmen together must include at least four representatives each of education authorities, universities and teachers, two Church of Scotland representatives and two Directors of Education. This leaves two to five members whom the Secretary of State appoints at his discretion, the Scottish Council having twenty-five members altogether.

The existence and composition of the Scottish Council give the Secretary of State [though not essentially appointed to administer education] much greater authority than the Minister of Education has in England. Whether one considers this a good thing depends partly on one's opinion of the Secretary of State and of the Scottish Education Department.

As regards the work done in the Colleges of Education and the way in which it is done, there are several important differences with England. The four main Scottish colleges are much larger than most teacher training colleges and Departments of Education in England, and put on a greater variety of courses. All four are mixed and mainly non-residential whereas many training colleges in England are single-sex residential establishments, with an unnatural atmosphere, especially in the case of women's colleges.

Finally a word as to the curious monopoly enjoyed by the Colleges of Education. There is nothing like it in Europe except possibly at Hamburg, where the University is responsible for all teacher training, but has a special department for primary teacher candidates, whereas intending secondary teachers take a degree with incidental training.

The reason for this monopoly is historical: the Universities refused to handle "vocational" training — apparently not regarding the degree courses in medicine, theology and law as vocational, although one emerged from them with a definite and exclusive working qualification. In England, where training was and is optional for graduates, the Dip.Ed. course developed a more "vocational" bias than it has in Scotland. It came into being as an "academic" course at a time when very few graduates bothered to train and then, as training came to be regarded as decidedly useful, began to embody teaching practice, lecturing in methods etc.

On the Continent there is, as in England, a clear break between the graduate and non-graduate sides of the profession, and this applies even in Communist countries. *Teachers* (primary, and sometimes junior secondary) are trained non-graduates, often completing their secondary education in the training colleges. *Masters* and *mistresses* in senior secondary and " semi-academic" secondary schools are graduates, usually with some training, but less than in Scotland. This training may form part of the degree course (Germany, Scandinavia, Communist countries generally) or may be given in a parallel course as in France, where students enrol at the same time in the Ecole Normale Supérieure and in one of the University faculties.

Whether this monopoly is a good thing I would not like to say. It may possibly make for greater unity within the profession than exists either in England or on the Continent. It may also encourage a more stereotyped attitude towards education itself and towards the subjects taught, and help to perpetuate the excessive formalism which I have already criticised elsewhere, but this attitude more probably springs from our character and traditions, as in Germany. On balance I am against it—but this may be my foreign background reasserting itself, though many Scotsmen with unimpeachable antecedents share my distrust of monopolies generally and of this one in particular.

The Universities could, I think, play a greater part than they have played hitherto. If we can avoid non-graduate " dilution " by setting up a three-year degree-cum-training course of the type I have suggested in Chapter VII, it would be their function to run this course—I don't like the idea of second-class Higher Education in a Liberal Arts College, which may be appropriate in America and tolerable in England, but will not do for Scotsmen.

At the risk of allowing " Chapter V" men and women to form a segregated *élite* I would also suggest that Universities, rather than Colleges of Education, provide the atmosphere in which they ought to be trained, as people of their calibre are trained everywhere else. New wine does not benefit from a sojourn in old bottles, and Scottish Education desperately needs new wine. At the same time I doubt whether the university bottles are new enough, and it is largely for this reason that I would like to see a fifth Scottish University built, to do a few of the jobs which the existing universities will not take on.

CHAPTER VII

Amenities and Personnel

Schools require both buildings and teachers. But good
teachers can cope in makeshift or obsolete buildings while the
glossiest of glass palaces cannot make up for the lack of competent
staff.

The general tendency has been, over the past few years, for
schools to have better buildings and fewer or worse teachers.

As regards buildings we are some way behind Germany and
Scandinavia, and a little behind England also. The reasons are
(1) German cities were largely destroyed during the war, and
have been rebuilt complete with up-to-date schools. The shifts
of population at the end of the war and the steady influx of East
Germans into West Germany have also caused a great deal of
fresh building as distinct from reconstruction.
(2) Over most of Scandinavia space is more readily available,
and the forests, into which new towns expand, are usually State
property in the first instance. This cuts down costs and helps
building all round—not only school building.
(3) England has generally had an expanding economy while
Scotland's has been mainly static and in places contracting.
Consequently English local authorities have had, on an average,
more money at their disposal, and there has also been more
reconstruction—following upon war damage on a larger scale—
more building of housing estates and of satellite towns. But,
while they have built more, what they have done has been done
more wastefully and not so well.

We are also paying the price for being first in the field. As
one Primary School headmistress told me, " many authorities have
been left a legacy of poor schools by their predecessors, and are
doing their utmost under difficult circumstances to improve the

condition of school buildings. Many of the new schools are non-traditional and give pleasure to the eye and mind of pupil and teacher alike, and this is reflected in the work done in such schools. Much remains to be done and much more money needs to be spent on them. Unfortunately teachers are seldom, if ever, consulted about the building of new schools. If they were, some obvious errors in pre-planning would be avoided."

I cannot altogether agree with her last criticism—it certainly does not apply in Fife, Renfrew or Roxburgh, probably not in several other counties. But it may well be valid for her own area, and it seems to me that teacher-participation in the planning of new schools ought to be mandatory, not left to individual authorities.

A further point is that it might be desirable to institute, at some of our universities, a course in architecture which also included some teacher training. Graduates of this course would then teach mathematics and/or science or art, part-time for three years, while also practising as architects. This would relieve some staffing difficulties and would ensure that, if planning schools at some future date, they should know all the problems and requirements particular to such buildings. Architects with this special qualification would be given preference over others whenever a new school was to be built.

Other criticisms have been made, both officially and un-officially. They are directed against:— (1) an excessive tendency to build " glass palaces " which are difficult to heat in winter and to cool and shade in summer, and (2) niggardliness in the allocation of square feet per pupil and of cost per pupil, which restrains imaginative building.

(1) Would I think disappear with mandatory teacher-participation, and the formation of architects with teacher-training and teaching experience.

(2) It is not essential that school buildings should be *imaginative*. What matters is that they should be adequate to their purpose, and that there should be enough of them. Neither objective has yet been reached, and there are more immediate priorities for the much larger budget which ought to be devoted to education as a whole.

As regards *teachers* we have lost our old commanding lead. The girls who come out of the Colleges of Education are—every-body assures me—as good as ever they were, but they rapidly marry and leave the schools: their expectation of teaching life is in the region of three years—no more, that is, than the time in which they are trained at the public expense.

Dedicated spinsters, the formidable backbone of the old-fashioned Scottish primary school, are a fast-vanishing race, and the campaign to recruit married women—in addition to those who were already in the schools a year or two ago—has not been a success. Meanwhile it becomes increasingly difficult to recruit suitably qualified men for the primary schools, bearing in mind that our formal qualifications for that category are far and away the highest in Europe — a complete secondary education, a university degree taken in three years, *and* a year's training.

At the top end of the scale, the Senior Secondary Schools are not recruiting the men of distinction who came to them in the 'thirties, when even a first-class graduate was glad to have a job. These men often went into teaching as a second, third or fourth choice in the lean years, liked it, and stayed; and many of them became the Rectors and Principal Teachers of today. They were an exceptional vintage — the conditions which produced them seem at present unlikely to recur.

What we are entitled to expect, and are not getting, are a sufficient number of highly qualified men, entering teaching for its own sake as a worthwhile career and way of life, and out of a deeply ingrained but unobtrusive spirit of service to the community.

Why is this?

One reason is the much greater demand for graduates, notably in commerce and industry, which formerly preferred to recruit at office-boy and shop-floor level. The salaries which teaching can offer may seem advantageous at the start—they are in no sense competitive for those aged 28 and above; and to those with family responsibilities, adequate salaries matter far more than ample holidays.

Another reason may be *lack of adult company*. This again puts off the middle-aged and the older teacher rather than the very young—but it is a future disadvantage which probably looms large when the student thinks seriously about a future career—and it may be that, at 20-22, young men are now more mature and more forward-looking than they were.

A third and possibly the most important reason is *lack of status*. This argument at present only applies to " State " schools, i.e. those whose staff appear on the pay-roll of a local authority, along with dustmen, sanitary inspectors, etc., and are as such excluded by statute from a place on education committees, and sometimes by regulation from taking any part in local politics.

It is because " Public School " and Grant-Aided school masters enjoy a better professional relationship with their employers, and higher status altogether, than " ordinary " school teachers, that these schools are still able to recruit men nearly as good as those who came to them in the Great Depression.

Other factors come into play—as over the whole of Europe. One of them is the disappearance of the old-fashioned " lad 'o pairts ", with an artisan or crofting background. The " lad o' pairts " was usually noticed, in the first instance, by the local schoolmaster and the minister or priest. They brought him on, and he not unnaturally became one of them. The present Pope is the most outstanding example. Stalin, Krushchev and Tito are others, but never went into the careers for which they were intended by any of their early sponsors, or started on them but did not stick to them. Very often they chose teaching as the career in which they would soonest begin to earn, and in which they would become natural leaders of the local community. This, in particular, was the way in which primary schools, often with a more or less secondary " top " recruited able, determined and dedicated men who could not afford to go to university. Secondary Schools also gained because the Arts course was shorter than the rest.

Lads (and lasses) o' pairts are now picked out by a more automatic process. They make their way up the Senior Secondary School to the University, with grants to support them, a wide choice of careers open to them, and no particular sense of obligation to an early benefactor.

The old breed is dying harder in Central and North Wales, North-Eastern Scotland and Norway than anywhere else, partly because of the lack of local or nearly-local opportunities outwith teaching, medicine and the Ministry—it is not every " lad o' pairts " however recognised and selected, who prefers prosperity in exile to a decent situation nearer home and the respect of those he has always known. In consequence much of Norway has an overall staffing ratio of 1 : 16 jointly with Russia's, the highest in the world—while many Welsh and North-Eastern teachers seek posts elsewhere for some years, returning home as vacancies occur.

The situation in Russia is quite exceptional. Many young men and even more young women sign on to teach for three years after graduation, simply in order to receive a higher education. All Arts graduates and 80% of other university graduates are required to teach for that period, while there is only room in the *universities* for about one-tenth of those who would like to attend them. Many therefore attend *colleges of education* instead, thus qualifying to teach in the first five grades of the unified primary/ secondary school: some of these colleges again have 7 to 13 applicants for one place—including I imagine, would-be students who apply for more than one college to increase their chances of getting in somewhere. Since this book will be read by some not familiar with the Scottish Educational system, I shall try to outline here the main teaching qualifications.

Primary School MEN: Teachers' General Certificate requiring an Ordinary Degree, obtained in three years, plus a year's course at a College of Education. *WOMEN* ideally as above, but the great majority of them have instead spent three years at a College of Education. Men are not allowed at present to qualify in this way.

Secondary schools: up to S.III: *men* and *women* teachers of general subjects (i.e. other than art, music, technical, rural and physical education).

As for primary school *men* above: but in addition the teacher should hold an " Article 39 " endorsement to his certificate. This entitles him/her to teach the particular subjects covered by his degree, diploma or other course.

Secondary Schools: *beyond S.III*: men and women teachers of academic subjects:

"Chapter V" or Teacher's Special Certificate. This requires an Honours Degree, taken in four years at a Scottish University, followed by two terms or a year in a College of Education.

Exceptional recognition may be granted in lieu of the above to teachers holding a similar English qualification—e.g. a three years Honours Degree plus a Dip.Ed. and satisfactory teaching experience. It is not given to untrained graduates.

Secondary Schools: teachers of Art, Music, Physical Education, technical subjects: rural subjects, domestic subjects.

These hold a "Chapter VI" qualification, in which the degree course is replaced by some other course regarded as a satisfactory equivalent for their particular subject. Depending on the atmosphere of the school they may be in a somewhat invidious position, not unlike that of sergeants in an officers' mess. For this reason it is particularly difficult to recruit teachers in this category.

Thus the percentage deficiency in these subjects in 1960, as given in the annual Report of the Secretary of State was:

Overall	16%
Handwork	5.3%
Homecraft	21.1% (due to high marriage wastage)
P. E. men	10.9%
P. E. women	14.4%
Art	13.7%
Music	29.1%
Commerce	22.3%
Other subjects (rural, technical)	15.8%

The only really severe shortages on the academic side were:

Article 39	Maths/Science	11.0%
Chapter V	Maths	15.9%
	Science	9.9%
	Geography	9.0%

The corresponding requirements in several other countries are given in my first book, "Schools of Europe". Very briefly they are as follows.

Primary School teachers are seldom *graduates* except in parts of Germany, where they take a three-year course which embodies teacher training. As a rule they have a complete secondary education[1] plus two years' training, or they complete their secondary education (in so far as they can be said to complete it) in teacher training schools (Iceland, Italy, Holland, France). They often, indeed usually, have some pupils who would be at Junior Secondary Schools in Scotland.

The equivalent of our "Article 39" teachers may be trained non-graduates or untrained graduates (England), university graduates with some incidental training worked into their course, and some teaching practice at times when schools are functioning while universities are not (German, Switzerland, France).

The equivalent of our "Chapter V" teachers may be incidentally trained graduates (Germany), Honours Graduates with or without training (England, Switzerland) or holders of a post-graduate qualification — the *agrégation* in France, the *lektorat* in Scandinavia. *Agrégés* and *lektorer* are not academic-

---

[1] By this I understand an education which would bring them, if of sufficient ability, to the level of attainment required for admission to a University in their own country.

ally equivalent to "Chapter V" but somewhat higher on an average. But the *agrégation, lektorat* and "*Chapter V*" respectively are the basic requirements for Headships of Schools and Departments in lycées, gymnasia and Senior Secondary Schools.

In countries where this higher qualification exists, its holders are fully on a level with doctors, lawyers and the clergy: they may combine school and university posts or alternate between them.

If we are once more to recruit men such as entered the profession in 1937-38, it might be desirable to create a qualification of this type, and place its holders on a really worthwhile salary scale, running say from £1000 to £2000.

To remedy the present shortage of men teachers in primary schools it has been suggested that non-graduates should be admitted to the Colleges of Education, as before 1924 and under the Emergency Training Scheme after the war.

This is open to several grave objections.

(1) The non-graduate men recruited in the past could have gone into the Universities but did not mainly for economic reasons. Non-graduates recruited now, when grants are so readily available, would be of lesser intellectual ability.

(2) While such men do a good job of teaching in England and on the Continent, it would be a mistake for the teaching profession here to lower its standards of entry when all others, and industry and commerce generally, are raising theirs. It would reduce still further the respect in which teachers are held, and could lead to embarrasssing situations when a non-graduate has in his class several children of graduate parents.

(3) Scottish primary schools retain "academic" pupils rather longer than those of most other countries.

(4) Non-graduate women, who admittedly do a good job, are historically a "necessary evil". At one time 90% of our women teachers were graduates. Now that so many of them marry so young, it is felt uneconomic to prepare them in four years for a teaching career lasting only three years on an average. But we hope that our men will stay in the profession until they retire while, if they don't, they ought to have a qualification of some use elsewhere. A degree is such a qualification: a teacher's certificate is not.

(5) One effect of admitting non-graduate women has been that many girls, academically qualified to enter a Scottish University, have chosen not to do so in order to start earning a

year earlier. The proportion of students thus qualified, but not taking a degree course, was recently found to be 50% at Notre Dame College of Education.

We may suppose that, with the prevailing desire to earn as soon as possible, a fairly high percentage of young men who now graduate would deliberately choose not to do so. With perhaps a 10% increase in the total number of men teachers we should get a 50% decrease in the proportion of graduates among them.

(6) It has up till now been Scotland's role to lead, not follow. What sort of example to other nations, not least England, would be the lowering of our standards of entry to the profession whose members prepare young people, ultimately for all other professions and occupations?

(7) We have hitherto been less snobbish than most. Do we want to set up the distinction between "professeur" and "instituteur" which exists in France and indeed nearly everywhere else? This would be the inevitable result of allowing a lower regular qualification for those who intend to make a lifetime career of primary teaching (which, as a rule, the non-graduate women don't).

We must look for other ways to fill the gaps in our schools. Among them I would suggest: —

(i) Much greater use of men who in the first instance only intend to teach for a few years. This would mean setting up a three-year degree course with incidental training and teaching practice. Such courses would serve as a qualification for teaching both in primary and in Junior Secondary Schools. A similar Honours course could be set up, qualifying teachers for Senior Secondary posts other than Principal Teacher. A course of this type is already the standard qualification in Germany, France and Scandinavia.

After three or four years those who had taken either of these courses would be encouraged to train for a further year and would then become fully qualified teachers in their respective categories.

The existence of the three year degree-cum-training course might also encourage many young women to take degrees, and a few to take honours degrees.

(ii) We should do more to make teaching an attractive occupation for suitably qualified *married women*. This would include reducing the hours worked by infants — in itself an excellent thing for them. For infant pupils whose mothers work, and for kindergarten-age children of married schoolmistresses, we should then set up establishments similar to the East German

"Hort" and again largely conducted by married women with a teaching or nursing qualification (see next Chapter).

(iii) There should be a substantial rise in salaries, coupled with some form of efficiency rating *not dependent on examination results* (since schools are not everywhere working under the same material conditions or with pupils with equivalent ability and parental backing) and probably with obligatory or "strongly expected" retraining, at reasonable intervals, for all teachers. I would suggest a month's course in every three years, with additional increments for those attending with success and an incremental bar for those failing to attend.

Existing salary scales are more than adequate for those who tag along doing the absolute minimum that is required of them. Such people are working barely half the hours at present current in most other occupations and enjoying far greater security.

The operation of this efficiency rating could be worked out and enforced by a strengthened Advisory Council, such as I have suggested elsewhere.

The sort of salary scales I have in mind, for those with full efficiency ratings and retrained at the appropriate intervals would be

Non-graduate women Ordinary graduates with incidental training }	£600-1100 in 12 years
Graduates with regular training	£660-1400 „ „ „
Honours graduates with incidental training Teachers of technical subjects etc. }	£750-1550 „ „ „
Honours graduates with regular training }	£850-1750 „ „ „
Lectors (with post-graduate qualification) }	£1000-2000 in 10 years.

Responsibility allowances etc. in addition to the above.

(iv) A qualification similar to the *lektorat* in Scandinavia should be instituted to attract men and women of real distinction to Senior Secondary schools. At some future date the rectors of these schools, and the Principal Teachers in the larger ones, would be expected to have this qualification (a combination of a First or Second Class Honours degree, three years' teaching experience or more and subsequent research leading to the publication of a thesis or other scientific work).

(v) The status of the profession as a whole should be raised by giving it much greater autonomy, under the aegis of the Advisory Council, and by disconnecting teachers from the ordinary run of local government employees. Their salaries should come straight from Edinburgh, and senior appointments should also be centralised or at any rate taken out of the hands of Education Committees or other lay bodies. These appointments could for instance be made by Directors of Education in conjunction with two members of the Advisory Council or other well-established headmasters. Lesser appointments could very well be made by the headmaster concerned, as in fee-paying schools.

Finally we should very seriously consider a much greater use of *part-time* and *extra-curricular* personnel as practised in Russia.

Russian "extra-curriculars" receive a form of teacher training in colleges of education. Their main sphere of activity is in youth organisations and "cultural centres" but they are also found on the staff of boarding schools and possibly (though of this, even after two visits, I am not sure) of day schools.

"Part-timers" are graduates or otherwise qualified teachers, who have justified their University or college places and grants by serving for three years as full-time teachers. Thereafter they may join a factory or other industrial concern, or become writers, journalists, interpreters and travel agency staff. But they continue to teach their speciality—maths, science, a technical subject or a language—for eight hours a week or so. Since the State is in any case their employer, it hardly matters in which way their time and talents are used, so long as it is for the good of the community.

Here certain salary and pension adjustments would have to be made but I see no reason why this could not be arranged, especially since it is in the interest of the firms releasing such persons that schools and universities should continue to send them leavers and graduates properly grounded in Maths, Science, etc.

We need a far more imaginative and less formal approach to these problems than we have shown hitherto. It has been our greatest weakness, especially when compared with the English, that we have insisted too much on the right paper qualification and not enough on the right people—that is on people who would communicate not only actual knowledge but also—and perhaps still more—the desire to learn and the ability to think.

CHAPTER VIII

The Extra-Curricular Side

The comparative shortness of this chapter in itself gives some idea of the traditional Scottish attitude to extra-curricular activities. Hitherto they have not been regarded as the business of public day schools, which existed purely to get their pupils through the curriculum, or as far as they would go.

In my travels I encountered several parents who still held the old view and many teachers and administrators who, while not holding it, recognised its tenacious survival.

Extra-curricular activities may be recognised under three headings.

(1) Activities largely taking place in classrooms, and in class time but not in any sense preparing pupils for an examination or qualifying them for their future careers. Many of these activities have quite properly become part of the curriculum (e.g. art, music) and are therefore mentioned in pupils' reports, either in their own right or as part of another subject—thus *drama* is now part of English in many schools if not most. There are still those who resent this trend, which has gone much further in some countries (e.g. the U.S.A.).

(2) Games, taking place in class time and on Saturday mornings, in day schools, and mainly between lunch and afternoon lessons in boarding schools. Public day schools are at a considerable disadvantage in that pupils need not be present at all on Saturdays, must usually be transported home at 4 p.m. on other weekdays, and often have part-time jobs.

(3) Clubs, societies, etc., generally meeting after school on weekdays. These can cover a very wide range of interests, and a few Senior Secondary Schools may have as many as forty of them. How far they flourish depends on many considerations.

Thus: (a) how high is the proportion of middle-class pupils in the school—these normally taking a greater interest in such activities than pupils with a working-class background?

(b) To what extent do pupils go in for part-time jobs?

(c) What proportion of pupils are dependent on *school* as opposed to *public* and *personal* transport?

(d) How far are the possible interests of these societies and clubs already catered for by existing youth organisations, etc.?

(e) How far is the school regarded as a *community*, how far as simply a *public utility*? This depends above all on the personality of its Rector.

(f) How keen are the staff and senior pupils?

The Americans allow activities coming under (3) in Britain to encroach to a considerable extent on the time-table, on the ground that they are in every sense as " educative " as the curricular subjects. A few experimental schools in England and on the Continent do likewise and for the same reason.

I do not think this would be practical here, for many reasons —essentially the lack of time, especially for " academic " pupils, and the deep-rooted hostility of both public and professional opinion.

There is a further argument which is that, where a well-developed local life already exists, it would be a tragedy to weaken it by concentrating within the school the " extra-curricular " interests of senior pupils.

The present staffing situation is in any case such that we could not follow American practice (not, in itself, very successful, and increasingly criticised by educationists and parents over there) with any hope of success. As it is we are very hard put to find teachers of art and music, or English teachers who can make a reasonably good job of " curricular " drama—the lack of suitable plays, especially for non-academic pupils, aggravates the situation.

If all teachers, whatever their curricular subjects, were also required to handle a variety of activities for which an " extra-curricular " atmosphere, with a minimum of enforced discipline, had to be maintained, it would become impossible to recruit and retain staff in the more " difficult " areas.

It is true that the Soviet Union manages to cope with the difficulty of recruiting adequate staff for curricular, semi-curricular and extra-curricular work, but conditions there are very different, as has been shown in the last chapter.

THE NEW KIRKCALDY HIGH SCHOOL AT DUNNIKIER.

What I have said about Scotland is largely true of all Europe West of the Iron Curtain and North of the Alps and Pyrenees, but with the following qualifications:

(1) Senior Secondary Schools in Scandinavia (including Iceland) are superimposed on Junior Secondary Schools, not parallel with them. This, and a very high proportion of boarders in some areas, enables them to maintain more of an atmosphere than is commonly found in this country. Moreover the great majority of their pupils have a middle-class background (Iceland is class-less but its population has an essentially middle-class outlook, tempered by many local peculiarities).

Consequently they develop a very wide range of activities, more often organised by the pupils informally than under the aegis of the school.

(2) In England the ethos and purposes of the Public Schools have had a considerable influence over the Grammar Schools and even some of the better "Secondary Modern" schools. There is a strong feeling, especially in small towns with a traditional and formerly independent Grammar School for boys, that it ought to go in for such activities and that masters and prefects ought to pull their weight in them.

As I have indicated elsewhere, there is considerable doubt as to what schools and teachers are for and in particular as to how far it is their business to develop character, build up the entire human personality, etc. If one accepts that they have such functions, how should they set about fulfilling a whole range of almost indefinable duties?

The general tendency is for teachers to play safe and stick to the curriculum. We try to be the right sort of people and to exert a helpful influence through the way in which we go about our appointed task, through the incidental conversation with pupils which arises in the course of our teaching and through the example of our day-to-day lives. If we are wise, we try to avoid being obvious — nothing is so ineffective as planned, deliberate and visible "character formation" imposed on those who not unnaturally prefer their characters as they are—especially when we can only stretch the bow-string for less than half their waking hours on barely half the days of the year.

So far as I can judge, the "character-building side" is much less in evidence here than in England or America. Less is said about it: much less is thought about it—in this we are more or less at one with the Scandinavians, the Germans and the French.

But our juvenile delinquency rate is not much more than half that of England and does not even begin to compare with America's. Perhaps that teachers who work hard and work their pupils hard have a stronger influence, simply by insisting on one extremely valuable habit, than all the daily assemblies, flag-raisings, speechdays etc. of our southern and western neighbours. On the other hand the English and Americans may in some ways be more " socially adjusted ". I shall return to this in the next chapter.

One argument often used both against extra-curricular activities and against the " character-building side " generally is that they tend to weaken home life and lessen the interest of parents in *their* educational functions.[1] How far is this true?

I think it applies to direct character-building in class time, and to the encroachment of " spare time activities " on such time. Parents in the first instance expect schools to teach class subjects in class time. Thereafter, if extraneous matter establishes itself on the time table, the parents eventually regard it as the school's job and lose personal interest in it. Manners, hygiene etc., become school subjects and parents cease to bother about them.

At the same time teachers in a day school know they can do but little to correct the influence of a bad or indifferent home, and therefore do not try very hard. " Bringing-up ", as distinct from " teaching " becomes a football ineffectually kicked about between home and school and in the end nothing gets done. This tendency has been observed in France (where public schools provide " moral instruction " instead of " religious instruction " for which parents arrange outwith school hours if they so desire). It has also been felt in England, perhaps still more in America.

On the other hand we have to remember there are many homes which are not merely bad, but as homes, virtually non-existent. If the schools make no attempt to bring up the children who " live " there, nobody will. What is the answer?

Perhaps we should look more closely at the East German institution known as a " Schulheim " or " Hort ." This is annexed to many schools but not part of it, and thus preserves the useful theoretical distinction between home and school. It serves those pupils who for a variety of reasons cannot return home as early as the others.

---

[1] Two of my critics said they had never heard of this argument. I have encountered it often enough—mainly advanced by irritated and strongly traditionalist parents, and to some extent by teachers also.

The " Hort " has its own personnel — women who have undergone a kind of teacher-training course but are not actually *teachers*. Their functions are to supervise the chidren's home-work, help them where necessary, but not too much, provide meals for them, supervise their rest period, and interest them in a wide range of games and activities.

Definitely *extra-curricular* activities, voluntary and occuring after school hours, have never in my experience known to *weaken* home life. On the contrary they strengthen it, because children and adolescents thus develop interests for which there was previously no scope in the home, and the parents in their turn become interested. They are especially valuable now that people have largely lost the art of entertaining one another within the family circle, strengthened by a few friends. It is through school clubs and societies, and the tidings of them brought home by the younger generation, that this art may perhaps be revived.

An interesting possibility would be the extension of inter-school activities, other than sports. Finland has made a remark-able experiment in this direction. Every Senior Secondary School (age-range 16-20 approx.) has a society whose activities are not unlike those of a University or College Union. These societies organise meetings and parties to accustom their members to public life. Between them they form two national associations (Finnish-speaking and Swedish-speaking, which hold annual meetings, conferences, study excursions and competitions in music, recitation and sports.).

We could perhaps also learn something from the subsidiary activities of Finnish schools. Apart from lending their premises, as in Scotland, for various local functions, they arrange courses, clubs and festivals for pupils who have already left, and they place their libraries and reading rooms at the disposal of local youth. All these activities are supervised by teachers, who receive extra payment for them, and in addition the schools may employ special youth service organisers.

The main obstacles to a successful development of the extra-curricular side are (apart from the prevalence of part-time jobs in some places), transport difficulties and lack of suitably qualified and interested staff who need *not* be teachers. Neither will be overcome unless we are prepared to spend a great deal more on education than we are spending at present. The *existing* educational budget is hardly sufficient even to provide for *curricular* education and the efficient performance by our schools and teachers of their traditional functions. How can we expect it to finance education in a much wider sense, with greatly enlarged purposes and many more subsidiary activities? Six per cent of the whole Budget and three per cent of the national income are spent on education, while nearly twenty per cent of the population are being educated in kindergartens, schools of all types, universities and " parallel establishments ". As I have asked before—what sort of sense does that make?

Conditions in Finland and over most of Northern Europe are not comparable to those prevailing in the Forth-Clyde industrial belt, in which three-fifths of us live. For this reason I think a bold departure is needed if we are to make a success of education in this wider sense. It is a departure that will also help to redress the economical balance of several counties, now gravely threatened or apparently doomed.

Large areas of Scotland, thinly populated but not unfit for human habitation, would provide an ideal setting for schools combining some of the features of Rannoch and Gordonstoun with those of an Outward Bound Course.

These schools would normally take pupils for the last term or year of the Junior Secondary course. They would have a fairly straightforward S.III curriculum though on a somewhat reduced scale to make room for other activities mentioned below. Their pupils would also take part in hill-walking, mountaineering, skiing and sailing expeditions, and they would provide certain services for the scattered local population, as Rannoch does: e.g. a fire brigade, an ambulance, and mountain, loch and sea rescue patrols.

The staff would consist partly of regular teachers with a special interest in this kind of work, partly of local people, especially on the technical and practical side, partly of teachers in " ordinary " schools, wishing a change from their normal routine, and very largely of young graduates not intending to teach for more than three years or so.

Such a network of schools would be fairly expensive to set up in the first instance, though a saving could be effected by building on a less ambitious scale than in the case of " ordinary " schools and by making, for instance, considerable use of timber pre-fabs and of two-tier and three-tier bunks. They need not be very expensive to run since, though healthy in all respects, they would not attempt to provide a high standard of living: as regards *food* they could be very largely self-supporting, provided

enough land were attached. In summer they could be transformed into hotels as are some of the Icelandic boarding schools,
and this would help them to pay their way.

Nevertheless they would certainly cost more *per pupil* than
Junior Secondary day schools. But so do approved schools, and
several times more. Public funds are only too forthcoming when
the adolescent has gone off the rails and needs to be guided firmly
back on to them. How much is spent on sensible prevention,
compared with the fortunes lavished on attempted cure?

At this point some mention should be made of the boarding
facilities provided by certain Highland counties, and notably by
Ross and Cromarty. They could equally well be discussed under
"Extra-Curricular activities" since boarding schools actually
organise such activities, while hostels enable "remote area"
pupils to take part in whatever is organised by the day school
which they attend—or under "Amenities and Personnel".

An extremely interesting booklet was published some years
ago by the County Council of Ross and Cromarty Education
Committee, under the title "Residential Education in Ross and
Cromarty". It is a report by Dr. George Thomson, who will
complete this year his quarter-century as Director of Education
for the County, and may be obtained from him at the Education
Offices, Dingwall.

While there has been some development since the booklet
was published, the main facts remain as stated.

Pupils who cannot return home daily, or can only do so at
considerable fatigue and inconvenience to themselves (and
expense to the County) may be accommodated in one of four
ways.

(a) in lodgings, receiving an allowance from the County,
equal to the cost of lodgings (as distinct from the whole cost of
boarding—it is taking welfare too far if parents actually have to
spend *less* on their children than if they had to feed them at
home);

(b) in hostels connected with a particular school but not
forming part if it, and not necessarily managed by members of
its staff;

(c) in School "houses" such as would be found in an
English-type Public School;

(d) in fully residential schools.

Method (a) has been found unsatisfactory from an educational point of view, and as expensive as (b) which is now standard for pupils attending junior or senior secondary schools and unable to return home daily, or able to return home but only at some inconvenience and sacrifice of educational opportunity.

Method (b) has many advantages cogently expressed in Dr. Thomson's report and not unlike those of boarding schools generally as given in Chapter V of this book. A useful by-product is that the hostels may be used for courses, conferences, and visiting parties of foreign pupils during the summer holidays.

Method (c) has not generally been adopted, as it is felt desirable that pupils should have a substitute for home life, distinct from their school life. In point of fact it is not easy to differentiate between a hostel, associated with a school and for the exclusive use of its pupils, and a " House " forming part of a boarding or day-and-boarding school. My view is that a " hostel " becomes a " House " if it is run by a master or mistress on the teaching strength of the school and if the discipline enforced there is that which would be imposed by a " strict " rather than an " average " parent.

Method (d) has been used in four schools each serving a particular purpose and alone of its kind in the County. These are :

(i) *Duncraig Castle School,* which provides a one-year course in domestic and general subjects for girls aged 14-17, with the possibility of a second year of more advanced instruction in these subjects, with Home Nursing and First Aid in addition, and a programme of character education through responsibility. As explained in Dr. Thomson's Report " Each second-year girl has a special duty which she is responsible for organising and carrying out. The second-year class also provides a School Captain and five prefects, who maintain the general discipline of the school; these positions are voted for by the second-year class."

(ii) *Balmacara House School.* This is run in conjunction with Duncraig Castle and provides one-year and two-year courses of practical and agricultural training, again with instruction in general subjects, for boys aged 14-17. The agricultural curriculum includes " the usual farm crops, management of beef and dairy animals, sheep and pigs, liming and manuring of soils, drainage and improvement of land, dairying and poultry-keeping, farm accounts, farm buildings, mechanics of farm machinery, working of the internal combustion engine and the electric motor . . . At certain times the basic curriculum may be interrupted to allow full-time participation in such operations as potato-planting, haymaking, silage-making, shearing and sheep-dipping, turnip thinning, and harvesting."

Both the above schools are situated near the Kyle of Lochalsh.

(iii) *Lews Castle College, Stornoway.* This is a junior technical college with the accent on navigation and the textile industry, but also providing courses in building and engineering. These courses may last one year or two years as above. In addition the College serves as a centre for day release and evening classes, some on its premises, others conducted by its staff in outlying villages.

(iv) *Raddery House, Fortrose.* This is a Special Primary School for *educable* but *very slow* pupils with I.Q's in the 55-70 range. Most of them are boarders but there are also a few day pupils from the neighbourhood.

All four schools also take pupils from Inverness-shire and Sutherland, by arrangement between the three counties concerned.

I strongly commend Dr. Thomson's booklet to all those with a serious interest in boarding education for the " ordinary pupil " and indeed to all with a serious interest in practical and technical education.

Finally I should add that my strictures on County Education Committees generally are not intended to apply to Ross and Cromarty where somewhat exceptional conditions prevail. The County does not include a single private school—while much of its territory has been alienated to foreign sportsmen, they are only in residence for very brief periods and it may safely be assumed that they do not sit on any if its councils or their committees. Everyone on the County Education Committee therefore, is to some extent at least a product of its schools, and most members are also parents of children in these schools. Furthermore the traditional Scottish respect for education has been fully maintained, as may be seen from a glance at the statistics of "Education in Scotland in 1960" (H.M.S.O. Edinburgh, 7s.) Thus nearly 15% of all pupils complete the Senior Secondary five-year course, as against 11% for Scotland as a whole, 9% for Lanark and just under 5% for Midlothian. 54% leave at the minimum age, as against a national average of 70% (Lanark 78%, Midlothian 83%).

Neither the "County set" nor the industrial working class are comparable in numbers or in relative strength to their brethren in southern Scotland, and the proportion of self-employed is far above the national average. There is also rather more in the way of religion and less in the way of "canned entertainment" than may be found in those areas where the great majority of Scotsmen live.

This being so it is not too difficult to find, thirty men and women, other than serving teachers, who know something about education and care about the way their schools are run.

CHAPTER IX

The End Product

This is a difficult chapter for me to write, as I have only
been teaching for seven years, and only one of them in Scotland.
It would be of uncertain value even if written by an older and
more experienced man, because of the natural tendency to
regard those who follow us as a degenerate breed. It has been
so ever since Socrates was accused of corrupting the youth of
Athens; it was probably so for generations before.

Nevertheless I must make some attempt to evaluate the "end
product" of our schools—in other words the adolescents who
leave them at ages varying between fifteen and eighteen—simply
because there is no other way to assess whether the schools are
doing their job. I can claim one qualification for sticking my
neck out—a passing acquaintance with young people in every
European country except Albania, Hungary and Rumania.

We must always remember that all those who leave our
schools are also—and probably to a greater extent—the products
of their homes and of the local community. Consequently,
though the structure of the education system, the subjects taught,
and the type of teachers are essentially the same, one will find
considerable differences between school-leavers at any particular
stage, in different parts of the country. You will not find the same
type of 15-year-olds in Shetland, South Uist, Glasgow and the
Borders; among Senior Secondary leavers the differences may not
be so great because the system will have had a further two years
to exert its unifying influence and because the Islanders will
most probably have been away from home for some time.

This, of course, applies with equal force to France, Norway,
Italy and all other countries in which strong local differences
exist and the national character and outlook are mainly embodied
in the educated middle class.

137

Bearing all this in mind I shall try to give my impression of those who emerge from our schools.

(1) *Junior Secondary*. These, except in certain remote areas, have the usual outward trappings of "teen-culture". They jive, they play "pop" records in coffee bars, the girls make themselves up at an absurdly early age. The likes of them are to be seen from Rome and the Pyrenees to Hammerfest, and from the Atlantic to the Iron Curtain and beyond. If one looks beneath the surface one may find certain important differences with England, certain similarities with the rest of Northern Europe and characteristics which may be regarded as distinctly Scottish and possibly developed by the schools rather than elsewhere.

In this country as in Scandinavia, most boys have always known some girls and nearly all girls have always known some boys. This is not true to the same extent of England, still less of most Continental countries, and it puts Scotland at a very definite advantage. Irresponsible and sometimes tragic love affairs ending at the best in unsatisfactory marriages, at the worst in suicide, are much rarer here than in England—perhaps because young people *can*, if they really want, marry without their parents' consent. Divorce, especially among those who marry young, is much rarer too. Courtship hardly seems to unbalance young men as it does in other countries, and this may help to explain why Scots get their feet on all sorts of ladders quite early and then keep climbing steadily. Scotswomen appear to make better mothers than most.

There is also — but perhaps I am mistaken — a greater tendency for young people to be thankful that they have a job and to stick to it. This could be due to more effective discipline a school—more probably to the greater initial difficulty in finding employment and to the risk of remaining unemployed for some time if one loses one's job or gives it up recklessly.

Moral standards as a whole—and morals do not exclusively revolve round sex and one's attitude to it—are higher in this country than in England, if the statistics for juvenile and adult delinquency are any criterion. Here the schools may claim some credit. In the first place they teach religion more effectively, not being bound by an 'Agreed Syllabus'. Secondly,—and this is probably more important—they make no attempt to do the parents' job for them. Parents know what to expect from the schools and what is expected from themselves, and this division of labour, though it presupposes a fairly narrow view of "education", has the merit of being effective. Unfortunately, there are parents who will not do their job, even though they cannot, as in England, claim the excuse that the schools are supposed to do it for them. Their children will grow up more neglected than they would have been in England, since it is impossible for teachers to start educating the whole personality of some children while only "teaching" others.

As compared with Scandinavia we show up rather badly in some ways, not because of our schools but because of our physical geography. Every Scandinavian adolescent lives within an hour's walk or twenty minutes' cycle ride of open country or the sea, or both. And the open country, except in Denmark, really is open. It is public property, offering unlimited scope for adventure of every kind—boating, camping, skiing, hiking, climbing. Full use of these vast free amenities is made—by boys and girls together. This involves some sacrifice of "morals" in the narrow sense but tremendous gains in other directions—health, resourcefulness, acquaintance with natural beauty and worthwhile outlets for super-abundant energy.

(2) *Senior Secondary*. Most of the above considerations apply. I would add some further points of comparison with England and with Scandinavia:

Young Scots have hitherto been not only better able, but more anxious, to get their feet on the ladder and keep climbing —less prepared than the English to go in for such activities as "Voluntary Service Overseas" which takes a year out of their regular working lives but would give them a unique and un-repeatable experience of self-education in completely different surroundings.

As compared with Scandinavians, and for that matter Germans, they are less mature in various ways. Twelve years of schooling do not give the same value between 5 and 17 as between 7 and 19, and in fact Scandinavians and Germans often have 13 years (7-20 or 6-19.) Nor are seven years' primary, and five years' secondary education worth the same as four years followed by eight, since secondary education involves contact with several adult minds.

My estimate is that primary school years should be counted as one "educational unit" each, secondary school years below the age of 16 as one and a half units, and thereafter as two units. That being so, Scottish senior leavers receive 15 or 17 "educa-tional units" while Germans have 19 and Swedes 20. "Public

School " boys, whose secondary education begins in the preparatory school and whose Sixth Form years must all count double, even if they begin at 15, are exposed to about 18-20 " educational units ".

Furthermore, the long summer holidays in Scandinavia and Germany enable Senior Secondary pupils to take very profitable seasonal jobs, worth up to £80 a month while they last. This makes them rather independent and in their last three years they often travel abroad under their own steam. Relatively few pupils in S.V. and S.VI have done so here, the great majority of Germans and Swedes in the corresponding forms—Unterprima and Oberprima; Ring III and Ring IV have done so—and this is true even of Swedes living 600 miles from any non-Scandinavian place (they do not count Denmark, Norway or Finland as " Abroad ").

Scottish leavers also give the impression of being less sophisticated—having less poise and " interviewable personality " than English boys and girls of the same age. This is due mainly to the different emphasis in the last years of the secondary course —on the acquisition and exposition of knowledge here, on ability to think and fluency of expression there. Since our young people may have greater competence all round, and usually have greater persistence, employers are willing to allow for this at an interview unless the job is one for which " interviewable personality " is in itself an essential qualification, as in advertising and in the sales and public relations side of many firms. One unpleasant feature of life in the 1960's is that there are many such jobs. I have far greater respect for the other more solid qualities, but perhaps we shall have to develop this rather despicable front-window artistry a little more than we have done hitherto. More, certainly, should be done to encourage the ability to think.

Whether the " end product " is getting *better* or *worse* is extremely difficult to establish. The only people qualified to give an opinion are those who have watched leavers fairly closely over a period of thirty-five years or more—long enough, that is, to experience the comparative prosperity of the 1920's, the Great Depression, the war years, and the post-war years, which at times look so much like becoming another pre-war. But these people are themselves affected by a natural tendency to think that young people are not what they were in the old days.

My impression—after taking as many opinions as I could and making due allowance for this tendency—is that there has been no marked deterioration overall—only changes, some for better, others for worse. For instance, the standard of spelling has gone down, if the complaints made by employers are to be believed, but young people may have a wider vocabulary when they leave school. There is perhaps less consideration for one's elders, but since children are no longer so unpleasant to each other as they were in my time (twenty-odd years ago) adolescents probably emerge without such a heavy load of resentment and are —apart from a criminal minority—more pleasant and helpful all round. Those virtues which serve in an emergency—courage, physical and moral endurance, determination to win through, etc. have in no way been eroded by higher standards of living and the greater availability of "canned entertainment". On the contrary, the opportunities to display them are ever on the increase as more and more young people take to the hills and the sea; and this is true not only of Scotland but of nearly the whole of Europe, except where standards of living are so low that there is no surplus of time or energy left for adventure and the testing of one's strength and skill.

CHAPTER X

Conclusions and Recommendations

The state of Scottish Education leaves no room for complacency, but as yet gives no cause for despair.

There are many essential tasks which our schools accomplish better than most others, and a few points where we retain our old supremacy.

Our system is basically *fair*. Without deliberately weighing the scales in favour of working-class and crofters' children, it gives them a better chance than they have in any other Western country, with the possible exception of Norway. (Iceland cannot be taken into account as it is the only *genuinely* classless state in existence at the moment.)

At the same time efficiency is not sacrificed to " democracy " to the same extent as in Norway or the Communist countries. This sacrifice involves three elements in Norway—an excessively late transfer age (14), admission to secondary school on the sole basis of the primary school class teacher's report, and teaching of Landsmal (the Norwegian equivalent of Scots) to the considerable majority of pupils whose written language is Riksmal (the Norwegian equivalent of Standard English). In Eastern Europe it involves the total absence of streaming right up to the Leaving Certificate and, in several countries, class quotas enforced against " bourgeois " would-be students.

Except where classes are decidedly oversize, and sometimes even there, normally intelligent children emerge from our primary schools thoroughly grounded in the basic subjects. This cannot be said of England, where transfer takes place a year earlier: if it can be said of Germany, Switzerland and France, which also have an early transfer age, that is because, in these countries, the less able pupils remain in the primary school to the end, and the proportion of pupils regarded as " less able "

142

is considerably higher than that of " age-promoted " Modified pupils in this country.

A further advantage of our system is that, except in the cities, pupils of various home backgrounds and intellectual ability need not part company until the age of 14 or 15—depending on whether they pass from a primary school to a junior secondary school with an academic stream (e.g. Jedburgh, Tomintoul, Laurencekirk) or to a Senior Secondary school with non-academic streams (Hawick, Galashiels). Over most of Western Europe this division is made when academic pupils leave the primary school, that is at 10, 11 or 12.

Class and language barriers, though they exist, are therefore not so sharply defined as in England, France or Germany. At the same time we are spared the artificially maintained uniformity of Communist lands, beneath which the old social Adam is constantly struggling to the surface, and not without success.

This makes us a more friendly people, a fact which Continentals readily acknowledge when they arrive here from England. I for instance use the Broadcasting House dialect, having been educated furth of Scotland. But here I am never conscious of the latent hostility which surrounds " U-speakers " over much of England—notably in all but a small fraction of London, in the East Midlands and the industrial areas of the North.

The organisation of our school system and of the secondary curriculum, and the spirit in which our schools do their work, also give us many points of contact with Scandinavia and with most Continentals. These will be of increasing value in the years to come—but to take full advantage of them we should teach a language to a much higher proportion of secondary pupils— perhaps 70% instead of 30%. Since Germans, " Beneluxians ", Frenchmen and Scandinavians alike now learn English as their first foreign language, we should multiply points of contact with them by teaching a choice of first foreign languages—probably French or German to academic pupils and Riksmal or Swedish to the rest.

So much for the credit side—inadequate perhaps but in no sense to be despised.

The debit side includes the following items:

(i) *Excessive formalism* and *lack of imagination* both as regards the qualifications to be held by teachers and the way in which most subjects are taught.

In this connection I cannot do better than to quote from Lord Ferrier's reply to my synopsis.

"I feel myself that the community is running the risk of being 'taken for a ride' by the educational experts, who, by insistence on examination successes, degrees, etc., wear out the young people, especially those who are not good at examinations and are creating a caste system of 'heaven-born' by treating a Degree as the only passport to success instead of as a yardstick of attainment to date."

While I am not in full agreement with Lord Ferrier, (a degree, after all, is useful evidence that one has spent three or four years in a highly civilised atmosphere as well as reached a satisfactory academic standard) I think he is, in the main, right and most of the *real* experts, as opposed to those who pass themselves off for such, would agree with him: several even go further.

We should certainly pay far, far more attention to personal qualities. Among the most important, in any schoolmaster, are (a) ability to make young people *want to learn*, (b) ability to put across a wide and worthwhile experience of life, as well as the curriculum subjects and the conventional virtues and attitudes.

Perhaps the greatest merit of the English and English-type "Public Schools" is that they generally recruit men who have these qualities.

(ii) *Lack of incentive* for teachers of real distinction, and *excessive security* for certificated teachers who only do the minimum required of them, and do it without any real feeling for their pupils or their work.

(iii) *Lack of attention* paid to the ablest 5% and the least able 15% approximately.

(iv) *Inadequate liaison* between Senior Secondary Schools and Universities.

(v) *Indecision* regarding the purposes of secondary education in this country. If the schools only exist to *teach* children and adolescents, whom parents and the local community *bring up*, far, far more should be done to remedy the defects outlined above.

If their purposes are to be more widely interpreted, as now seems to be the official theory, then we must strike out boldly on the "extra-curricular" and semi-curricular" side. This means lengthening the school day by two hours and providing all sorts of facilities which at present hardly exist, save in a few experimental schools. We must have House Rooms, not normally used for teaching, except of Sixth Form groups, and provided with libraries, table-tennis, hobby outfits and indoor games. The practice of dining in schools must be more strongly encouraged, and the regular presence of all teachers required—in effect dinner must become part of the daily time-table rather than a welfare service laid on for those who cannot conveniently return home.

I do not accept the official theory, so far as day schools are concerned—though I should like all pupils to have some experience of boarding school life at some stage in their career. *But those who accept it must accept its implications,* among them a much higher level of public expenditure on education: 100% certainly and probably 150% to 200%.

What we spend *now* is only just adequate to the traditional and essential tasks of our schools, and several countries, where no more is attempted, are spending much more—Switzerland and Holland for a start. If academic work is only half of what the school has to do, it follows that what we are spending is only half of what we ought to spend. The "extra-curricular" work cannot be accomplished without the same teachers better paid, or more teachers, or preferably both, nor without additional indoor and outdoor space and equipment.

These criticisms in themselves indicate some of the reforms which are urgently required.

But these reforms cannot be carried out within the framework of the existing *political* and *administrative* set-up. They pre-suppose more power for those who know more about education and less for those who know less. The authority of the Scottish Education Department (or whatever may replace it in a more independent Scotland), of Directors of Education and of individual headmasters and educational bodies must increase—that of people relatively unfamiliar with education generally and Scottish Education specifically must decrease.

Going from top to bottom the following changes *at least* must be made.

(1) The legislature ultimately controlling Scottish Education must be purely Scottish. Ideally it should be a Scottish Parliament. As a temporary expedient it could be the Scottish Grand Committee *minus its "makeweight" Englishmen* and *meeting in Scotland* to deal with this and other Scottish issues. This would mean retiming the activities of the Westminster Parliament in such a way that matters of "British" interest should not be transacted on the first two, or alternately the last two days of its working week, unless in an emergency. In an emergency the Westminster proceedings would be relayed to Edinburgh and Scottish M.P.s could divide there, and have their

votes and abstentions transmitted southwards and added to those of their English, Welsh and Ulster colleagues.

(2) All educational finance must be centralised in Edinburgh, whether or not we become independent enough to have a Budget of our own.

Assessments for rates, the level of local taxation, and the rents payable for council houses should also be decided there. This would make it impossible for certain authorities to ingratiate themselves with local electors either by charging absurdly low rents or by holding the rates down, to the probable disadvantage of education in either case.

Local taxation would then be locally levied but in accordance with principles centrally laid down. The central authority, whatever its name, would collect the educational slice, and would add it either to the educational slice of the Scottish Budget, or to the educational slice of the Treasury grant made to Scotland as a whole—depending on the extent of our independence at the time.

It would be for the Scottish Parliament, or the Scottish M.P.s meeting in Edinburgh on two days a week, to decide how much of Scotland's financial resources should be spent on education, and on the broad outlines of how it should be spent.

Either of these legislative bodies would act as a far more satisfactory focus of responsible Scottish opinion than the Westminster Parliament — remote and over 80% English — or local authorities elected on a very indifferent poll—often in the region of 20-30% and largely consisting of very indifferent persons— nice, decent, honest people to be sure, but neither individually nor collectively the voices of the nation.

In consequence we could reasonably hope that a larger share of Scotland's resources would be spent on education, and that it would be spent more intelligently and to greater effect.

(3) At the next level two reforms are essential — more competent local authorities and more powerful Directors of Education. The second reform would probably follow from the first, without any change in their constitutional position or functions. Education Authority members elected solely for that purpose would I think be more inclined to recognise an administrator who knows his business and less likely to obstruct him on grounds of prejudice or political bias. It is for this reason that administrators who remember the old authorities all prefer them.

The former danger inherent in *ad hoc* bodies, that of domination by the Church or Churches, has almost entirely disappeared, except in counties where religion is still such a powerful influence that it can dominate local politics as a whole, not merely the educational sector.

Ad hoc city and county authorities, especially with only 12 or 15 members instead of the present 24-30 (and sometimes considerably more) would contain a much higher proportion of people with not only a strong *interest* in education, but with *definite* and *up-to-date* knowledge of what goes on. This would especially be the case if teachers were eligible to these authorities, as they are in Norway.

If teachers were neither appointed nor paid by these authorities, there would be no reason why they should not be eligible. Should any other issue arise, in which they had or could have a personal stake, they would be expected to declare their interest and abstain from voting. They should not, however, be expected to refrain from taking part in the discussion, since it might very well happen that their contribution would have been the most relevant. An alternative to *ad hoc* authorities was suggested at this point by Lord Lothian—namely representatives of (a) parents (b) teachers elected to County Education Committees as at present constituted. They might be acceptable subject to three qualifications.

(i) The total number of Education Committee members should not become larger as a result and should in most cases be reduced. 24 may be tolerable: 50 certainly is not.

(ii) Parents' representatives should be elected by *all* parents on some sort of ballot, *not* by parent-teacher associations, which may easily fall under the domination of a militant caucus.

(iii) Teachers' representatives should be elected as above by all teachers, not by organisations.

(4) I am opposed to any merging of counties into educational "provinces", as proposed by some of the well-known people whom I consulted. The financial advantages would not be considerable if, as I suggest, all educational finance is in any case centralised. Nor, if one halves the size of education committees and transforms them into *ad hoc* bodies, need there be any shortage of local people qualified to undertake whatever responsibilities continue to be local.

This "reform" would have three unfavourable effects at least.

1. Lack of incentive to potential administrators. There would only be nine or ten Provincial Directors, instead of thirty-five City, County or Joint County Directors.

2. Lack of contact between Directors of Education and the schools they administer.

3. Lack of consideration for local feeling and local conditions.

In fact — if all education were centrally financed — there might be a very strong case for creating a new education area comprising the Western Isles parliamentary constituency and with a substantial majority of native Gaelic speakers. At present this area — for all purposes other than Parliamentary — is divided between Inverness and Ross and Cromarty.[1]

(5) As I have said before, Secondary School Rectors should normally be responsible for selecting their staff. This is informal practice in Fife at least, and probably in several other counties. It should be made statutory. They should also have the right to buy textbooks and equipment, within a reasonable limit of expenditure, at other than " requisition times ".

Senior appointments should be made by Directors of Education with the advice of two members of the Advisory Council, or alternately of two Rectors, one within, one outwith the area. They should probably be required to make a reasonable proportion of such appointments from teachers outwith the area, and encouraged to appoint a far higher proportion of fairly young Rectors and Principal Teachers than some of them do at present.

There is no such thing as a moral right to a promoted post. Rectors and Principal Teachers should be appointed not as a reward for past service but for the good they seem likely to do. Automatic promotion and closed shops breed complacency or despair depending on whether one feels securely established on the ladder, or whether one has apparently missed the 'bus. They have no place in such a vital public service as education.

(6) I have repeatedly mentioned the Advisory Council in the course of this book. Having met or corresponded with several of its members and read most of its post-war reports, I am convinced that it deserves a more permanent status and greatly increased powers.

---

[1] In such circumstances several other areas might well be reorganised. Thus rural South Lanarkshire (the Upper Ward) could become an education area of its own, or be joined with under-populated Peebles-shire. Eskdale might be detached from Dumfries, and Liddesdale from Roxburgh, to form a new " Langholmshire ", and so on.

Transformed to the extent of including perhaps 50% or 60% of members elected by the profession at various levels, it could and should become the supreme governing and disciplinary body of Scottish Education: the counterpart of the Conseil Superieur in France,[1] the Educational Council in Holland, and a number of similar bodies, with more departmentalised functions, in Norway (see Olav Hove, *Outline of Norwegian Education*, obtainable from the Royal Ministry of Church and Education in Oslo).

It would advise the Scottish Education Department (or whatever takes its place) on all educational legislation, all major developments in policy and adminstration, all other matters on which it was asked for advice, and all matters which it chose to give advice. Except in this last instance, it would be entitled to have its advice taken.

It would also have final jurisdiction in the following matters: —

(i) Closure of public (i.e. " State ") schools on the grounds of economy.

(ii) Closure of improperly conducted independent schools, as provided for in the Education (Scotland) Act, 1945.

(iii) Withdrawal of grant from grant-aided schools.

(iv) Dismissal of teachers and Heads in the public service (including grant-aided schools) and of Directors of Education and other administrative personnel.

(v) Withdrawal from unsuitable persons of the right to teach in public and grant-aided schools.

(vi) Withdrawal from grossly unsuitable persons of the right to conduct, or teach in, any school in Scotland.

(vii) Disqualification of such persons from any sort of employment connected with education in Scotland.

A further responsibility of the Advisory Council, or one of its sub-committees, might be to conduct a kind of *Staff College* for people on their way to becoming Headmasters, Directors of Education and Lecturers in Education at University and Colleges of Education.

Outstanding personal qualities as well as academic merit would be looked for in those entering this Staff College. Its diploma would not be essential for the higher posts, but a powerful added qualification. There would be a common course

---

[1] The Conseil Supérieur in France is the Supreme *disciplinary* body. It is not exactly the supreme *governing* body but it is consulted in all important matters and, since it is more permanent than the Minister or his "Cabinet" its views carry a great deal of weight.

with options for the three categories of educationists mentioned above, and much time would be spent, as at the Army original, in working out problems on a group basis, with some members from each special course.

Entry would be at Principal Teacher, Depute Director or Assistant Lecturer level and the course would last one year. Stirling is the site I have in mind. To help finance this scheme and broaden the atmosphere of the College a few places could be sold to English and Scandinavian authorities.

(7) Regarding structural reform of the schools themselves I am only prepared to comment on one point.

I do not think that the Icelandic arrangement whereby *all* pupils go to a primary school followed by a junior secondary school, a minority then going on to a senior secondary school, would be practicable here, except in the cities and a few large burghs, where it might have much to commend it. Edinburgh is making an experiment along those lines but its validity is impaired by the commanding position which the fee-paying schools have built up: the Leicestershire Experiment follows similar lines, as do new arrangements in Fife.[1]

To work effectively, it presupposes a higher starting and maximum leaving age, with transfer at 12 and 15 or 16, and Senior Secondary pupils remaining to the age of 19: it might also work with transfer at 11 and 14/15, and Senior Secondary pupils habitually remaining at school until 18 (which, in itself, might be well worth encouraging). But sections of 7, 3 and 2 years respectively in a three-tier system would not be reasonable. The Icelandic sections consist of 5 or 6, 3 and 4 years respectively: summer holidays last four months (and Senior Secondary pupils nearly all have summer jobs — 85% of them are fully self-supporting. This makes a very late senior leaving age more acceptable, especially as the national economy is highly seasonal).

The social price paid for these arrangements is that Icelandic senior pupils are, by our standards, excessively independent and that sexual morals in particular are virtually non-existent. But

---

[1] The Fife experiment involves (1) Primary Schools for all (2) Junior High Schools for all. These keep *highly academic* pupils for two years, moderately academic pupils to " O " Grade (four years) and non-academic pupils for three, possibly four years. (3) High Schools. Highly academic pupils join these after two years in Junior High Schools—others may join from Junior High Schools having taken " O " Grade. At present, however, more traditional arrangements will continue to operate in Kirkcaldy and in the area served by the Waid Academy, Anstruther.

that is the custom of the country and fully accepted by all concerned.

Where there exists a traditional "omnibus" Senior Secondary school, capable of taking pupils through the sixth-year course (which I think we must now regard as standard) it should be left untouched.

Where there exists a similar school capable of taking pupils through the five-year course, but unable to run a sixth year, it should also be left untouched. Pupils intending to go on to Universities should then join the preparatory department of a university and remain there for a year, subsequently joining (if successful in the preparatory course) those who arrive from six-year schools.

Where the traditional "omnibus school" now loses its academic pupils after two or three years it should retain them for a fourth year to provide leadership within the school and an incentive to able teachers to come or remain there.[1] After four years they would take "O" Grade or an alternative examination entitling them to bypass "O" Grade, and embodying rather less factual knowledge but more thought. They could then join the fifth year of a six-year school, or the first year of a University Preparatory Course, rejoining six-year pupils after two years, if they qualify for the degree course itself.

I feel it is of the utmost importance, even at the price of some efficiency, that the educational self-respect of our small and medium-sized burghs should be maintained. Who destroys them destroys Scotland.

It is also of the utmost importance that the distinctive character of our country and nation should be maintained and where need be restored. We should not expect it to stagnate: on the contrary it must evolve, but along its own lines. We must remain ourselves and we must remain different. I am willing to subscribe to the proposition that "There'll always be an England" but only on condition that there shall always be a Scotland. We have our distinctive contribution to make to Europe and mankind, as we have made it in the past—but to continue making it we must continue to be Scotsmen, not a poor imitation of something else.

For details of the Scottish contribution I must refer my readers to Dr. George Davie's "The Democratic Intellect", an

---

[1] Laurencekirk (Kincardineshire) has "recovered" its academic side, up to the fourth year in this way.

expensive but very worthwhile book (Edinburgh University Press, 50s.). In my view the essence of that contribution is that we have made liberty, equality and fraternity more of a reality than any other nation of comparable size. The old Caledonian chord vibrates from Galgach—Agricola's defeated but undaunted opponent—through Wallace, Bruce, Barbour and many more to Robbie Burns and on to ourselves. In such as our fathers, and such as ourselves, the hope and sanity of civilization are enshrined.

We are also one of the very, very few peoples that have given women their proper place in society—free, yet honoured; equal, yet cherished; neither beasts of burden nor useless ornaments; and for this we have had, up till now, the women we deserved—second to none and way ahead of most.

These are the essentials—kilts and pibrochs are pleasing accessories. I think they are more than sufficient justification for maintaining our separate identity and for taking any steps necessary to that end.

There is no *immediate* danger—for generations past Scotsmen have never felt so Scottish as they do today. Nevertheless there are many alarming signs. Various innovations and reforms give the impression of having being taken for the sake of conformity with England—for instance the introduction of the new *Ordinary Grade*. That particular reform was, in my view, justifiable in itself—so probably were several of the others—but I would have felt happier had they been introduced on the authority of a Scottish Ministry of Education finally responsible to a Scottish Parliament.

Ultimately I doubt whether our distinctive character can be maintained unless, within a Europe more united than at present, we make ourselves equal in status to the Norwegians, the Danes and the Swiss. Devolution such as Ulster enjoys it not enough —we must bear our own international personality. Scotland must be, as she was for centuries, one of the States of Europe, not simply included as part of Britain. Whatever independence we recover—and no one country will be as independent as it is now—must be ours by right, not conceded to us as an administrative convenience. Educational reforms along distinctive lines will not be enough to prevent absorption of the lesser by the greater.

This absorption must be prevented because " the lesser " have usually done more than " the greater " to make life worthwhile. Rome transmitted to us the culture of Athens—but the distinctive Roman contribution was not so breathtaking as the Athenian — though certainly essential to the preservation of both.

For this reason we must preserve and strengthen our direct connections with countries other than England—especially our old ally France, different though she is; Switzerland, whose character and traditions are so like ours, and our neighbours— Iceland, Norway, Denmark and Sweden; also with New Zealand, the other Scotland beyond the seas.

There are many ways in which this could be done, educationally and otherwise. The educational ways alone are my concern here. They include teacher and pupil exchanges on a much larger scale than at present—more widespread establishment of a correspondence between Scottish and Continental or Scandinavian schools, more extensive teaching of languages and a greater emphasis on European geography and history.

The connections with New Zealand—and with Nova Scotia— may be a little more difficult to maintain—but we must also find ways to maintain them, and anything we spend for that purpose will be well spent.

On this note I must end — two of the most important processes going on in the historical present are the uniting of Europe and the shrinking of the world.

I hope that Englishmen and others who have read this book know Scotland a little better, and that it has made us a little more concerned with her future, a future which depends very largely on the way her children are taught and still more, perhaps, on the personal worth of the men and women whose work is to teach them and whose life is to set them an example they will respect, and follow so far as they are able.

The ministers of the Kirk, the " heather priests " and the schoolmasters have, more than any other human influences, made Scotland what she is and Scotsmen what they are. The Kirk has lost much of its old authority and—though a Catholic—I feel more has been lost than gained. The priests are only maintaining their position—with an increased nominal following each year but a decreasing hold over those who claim or are claimed to belong. The Scottish Dominie and the Scottish Schoolmistress therefore bear a heavier weight of responsibility than ever before. Scotland must not let them down—nor dare she let them slide.

The Scottish Council For Research in Education

The Scottish Council for Research in Education was established in 1927 by the joint efforts of the Educational Institute of Scotland and the Association of Directors of Education in Scotland. It now enjoys the support not only of these bodies but of the Association of County Councils in Scotland, the Association of Counties of Cities in Scotland (Glasgow, Edinburgh, Dundee, Aberdeen), the Scottish Education Department, the Scottish Council for the Training of Teachers, the Scottish Universities and Colleges of Education, the Scottish Branch of the British Psychological Society, the Association of School Medical Officers of Scotland (all these being represented on its Council) and of several Grant-aided schools. The Local Education Authorities contribute on a yearly basis of one penny per pupil, though some give rather more—thus Banff contributed at more than three times the above rate in 1960-61. Their total contribution in that year was slightly above £4,000. Local and District Associations of the E.I.S. contributed £114-5-0 in that same year, on a very uneven basis—thus Roxburghshire gave £10, the same as Fife, and nearly twice as much as Aberdeen, which have six and four times its school population respectively.[1] The Grant-aided schools contributed just over £60.

The Scottish Council does what its title implies, within the limits set by its relatively narrow means. It carries out collective research projects—e.g. Surveys on Gaelic-speaking children in primary and secondary schools, on the value of nursery school education, and the retention (or loss) of basic English/Arithmetic skills by "minimum-age" leavers. It also provides advice, lends rare works of reference, and in other ways assists individuals

---

[1] The E.I.S. as a *national* body, however, made a much more substantial contribution (£1324).

carrying out worthwhile projects. Subject to stringent conditions and in particular to proof that *original documents have been faithfully consulted and accurately quoted* it undertakes publication of the results at no profit to itself or to the author.

Finally it co-operates with similar bodies furth of Scotland—e.g. in comparing the attainments of thirteen-year old children in a number of European countries.

The Council's address is 46, Moray Place, Edinburgh 3. Its Annual Report includes a list of extant publications and of others on their way.

APPENDIX B

*Experiments in Primary School Methods and in the
Teaching and Use of Gaelic*

The Drumlanrig Experiment

An interesting experiment is now in progress at Drumlanrig St. Cuthbert's School, Hawick.

The first three primary classes are unstreamed. P.IV and P.V have A and B streams. P.VI and P.VII, for subjects other than English and Arithmetic, constitute four classes of mixed ability. For English and Arithmetic they are divided into four sets based on ability. Thus Set 4 will consist mainly of slow P.VI pupils but may also include very slow P.VII pupils. Conversely Set 1 will consist mainly of the abler P.VII pupils but may also include very able P.VI pupils. (This is very rare: good P.VI pupils are usually in Set 2).

These sets are taken by the four teachers who also take the two unstreamed classes in P.VI and the two unstreamed classes in P.VII. It is therefore quite possible for the same pupil to be taught History and Geography by one of them, English by another and Arithmetic by a third, and this should make it easier for him to adapt to secondary school arrangements, when he will come into contact with six or more teachers as soon as he reaches S.I.

The daily time-table is partitioned off into four "blocks" separated by the dinner break and the morning and afternoon intervals. Pupils in P.VI and P.VII will only have class subjects or set subjects in any one block. Thus they may start the day with Arithmetic, followed after the morning interval by three periods of English. After the dinner break they may have History and Geography, and after the second interval they will finish the day with Art, in which they are taken as a class but by a visiting specialist.

Results so far have proved very satisfactory but this system could only work effectively in a large primary school. One of its advantages, from the point of view of the slower pupil, is that he need not be in a bottom stream all the time, since P.VI and P.VII are not streamed by ability in subjects other than English and Arithmetic.

There would be a strong case for its extension to secondary schools (at present it only exists in a few of the largest; e.g. Kirkcaldy High School). The basic difficulty here is that some subjects are at present only taken by academic pupils, others only by non-academic pupils; another point is that it may be in the best interests of the academic pupils to keep them together as a class, with an atmosphere and an *ethos* of its own, particularly if there are only just enough of them to form a class.

Experiments in the Teaching and Use of Gaelic

For many years Gaelic was not merely neglected but actively discouraged in the schools of Gaelic-speaking areas. At one time pupils could be punished for shouting a few words of their mother tongue across the playground. Gradually a more tolerant attitude prevailed and, in between the World Wars, the old language became a legitimate alternative to French in a few Senior Secondary Schools, and a possible subject for presentation on the Higher and Lower Grades of the Scottish Leaving Certificate. It was only offered by pupils who were " native speaking ", and the papers were constructed accordingly.

More recently, with the blessing of the Scottish Education Department and of the Scottish Council for Research in Education, two sets of experiments have been carried out.

(1) Gaelic is now taught for half an hour a day to all primary school pupils in those of the Western Isles which belong to Inverness-shire—i.e. Barra to Harris inclusive, but not Lewis. Some of these pupils are not " native speakers "—they may for instance be children boarded out with island families by the Glasgow Children's Officer, or their parents may be " incomers " from the mainland.

At the same time it is used as *a medium of instruction* in Geography, History, Nature Study and Religious Knowledge. At present it cannot be used for the teaching of Arithmetic because not all the appropriate technical terms exist in Gaelic. This difficulty could be overcome by inventing suitable terms or by importing them from Irish.

It has been found that Gaelic speaking pupils taught through Gaelic score rather better in I.Q. tests and in the " Qualifying " examination as a whole than pupils who have been compelled to work through English from the start, and this even though the entire Qualifying procedure is at present conducted in English.

There would probably be a case for conducting the procedure as in Wales, where all pupils, except recent arrivals from England, take one paper in English and one in Welsh, while the I.Q. and Arithmetic tests may be attempted in either language. A young research student has recently conducted experimental I.Q. tests in Gaelic.

Two special difficulties arise in the " Qualifying " procedure as conducted in the Western Isles.

(a) The islanders have a poor sense of time, and their performance in timed tests is therefore not a true measure of their ability.

(b) The vocabulary of the tests includes trains and other objects which most island pupils have never seen and can only imagine with some difficulty.

The importance attached *to class teachers' reports*, however, goes some way to offset these difficulties.

Junior Secondary pupils in the Inverness-shire islands also learn Gaelic. Senior Secondary pupils may learn it on the islands for two years as an alternative to French, which is not taught there. They must then transfer to senior secondary schools on the mainland, where they may continue with Gaelic to Ordinary and Higher Grade. Pupils opting for French in S.I are immediately transferred to Secondary Schools on the mainland. I understand from the Headmaster of Lochaber Secondary School that " Knowledge of Gaelic is without a doubt helpful in the learning of any other language ".

There would be a strong case, for teaching French through the medium of Gaelic if suitable teachers could be found. This would involve the use of Direct Method textbooks, those explanations which are normally given in English being given in Gaelic instead. The two languages have many sounds in common and both have a more complex grammar than English.

(2) Gaelic is now taught in wholly English-speaking areas to secondary pupils, the majority of whom have English as their native tongue.

At Norton Park (Edinburgh) it is taught to "non-academic" pupils: at Woodside and Bellahouston (Glasgow) it is taught to "academic" pupils living north and south of the Clyde respectively, as an alternative to French. A few are "native speakers" —a greater number have a Gaelic-speaking grandparent or uncle in the Highlands or the Western Isles — many start entirely ignorant of Gaelic and having no natural connection with the Gaelic-speaking areas.

At Bellahouston the first and second-year Gaelic classes are unstreamed. In the third and fourth years there are "sets" whose work respectively leads up to O Grade Paper 1 (designed for "native speakers") and to O2 (for "learners"). At present there is only one Higher paper, designed for "native speakers" and exceptionally fluent "learners". Logically there ought to be an H² paper also.

One difficulty is the shortage of suitable textbooks: those which exist are designed for "native speakers" only. In my view the Scottish Education Department should take a hand, as the Ministry of Education has done in Norway, Sweden and Finland for the Lapps, and produce its own textbooks for this minority interest, bearing in mind that they cannot be a commercial proposition. Losses could be reduced to some extent by selling copies to adult learners and potential learners, especially tourists visiting Gaelic-speaking areas, and possibly by exporting copies to Canada, where Gaelic remains a fairly flourishing language in some districts—notably around Alexandria (60 miles west of Montreal) and on the Cape Breton peninsula of Nova Scotia.

A serious obstacle to the success of experiment (1) is lack of interest on the part of the islanders themselves. Many of them feel that the knowledge and use of Gaelic has been of no material use to them and, though speaking it among adults, will not speak or teach it to their children. The lack of opportunities on the islands has been very largely at fault—parents feel that their children will only have a future outwith the islands, and will therefore need fluent and natural English. They seem unable to appreciate that they are renouncing, on their children's behalf, a priceless and irreplaceable heritage.

Three remedies are urgently required: (i) a strong and persistent campaign to make them realise the value of what they are giving up and the impossibility of reclaiming it once it is lost.

(ii) An equally strong and determined drive to create more material opportunities on the islands and on the West Coast without having to import a large English-speaking population. The development of the seaweed processing industry on South Uist is a step in the right direction. Extension of Scottish territorial waters to the traditional twelve miles from headland to headland, and closure of these waters to all non-Scottish fishermen, would also help. In the immediate future it would mainly assist the East Coast fishermen but the West Coast and Islands would also benefit in due course.

(iii) Native Gaelic-speaking teachers, many of whom have high teaching qualifications in other subjects, should be encouraged to return to the West Coast and the Western Isles, not necessarily for their whole career, but at least for occasional spells of three to five years. Teachers who have learnt Gaelic from scratch, either at school or thereafter, should also be encouraged to serve for a time in areas where this knowledge is likely to be of practical use to themselves and to others. With that end in view the "remote area" and "Gaelic-medium" allowances should both be made more substantial than at present. This could only be achieved if all education were nationally financed since the Gaelic-speaking areas are among the least prosperous in Scotland.

School Hours (Approximate)

It may be interesting to compare the hours worked by school pupils in Scotland and in a number of other countries.

Scottish and English pupils are normally in school from 9 till 12 and 1-15 till 4 or thereabouts, Mondays to Fridays. The first afternoon period is sometimes transferred to the end of the morning, and an eight-period day is worked, with periods lasting thirty-five or forty minutes each. *Infants* usually work one period less in the afternoon and in a few schools they attend mornings only. Irish schools work a similar week but their day is half an hour shorter.

In France, Belgium, French-speaking parts of Switzerland, Portugal, Spain and Italy the dinner break is much longer, two hours and sometimes nearly three. French pupils normally attend five days, Saturday being a normal working day but Thursday free—in Senior Secondary Schools Thursday and Saturday are half-holidays for the older pupils. The other Latin countries work a 5½ day week (Saturday afternoon free), but their working day is a little shorter, 5½ hours rather than 6, and the total working week adds up to 30 hours approximately as in France, including recreation intervals but excluding the dinner break. On this same basis the British school week adds up to 28 hours approximately, depending on the time allowed for registration, etc.

All other European countries work the *extended morning*. This usually starts at 8 or 8-30 for all, but infants often leave at 11 or 11-30, other primary pupils at 12 or 12-30, Secondary pupils up to the age of fifteen at 12-30 or 1, senior pupils half an hour later. Exact arrangements vary; a six-morning week, however, is always in force. The working week therefore runs from about 18 hours for P.I. (aged 6 or 7, not 5 as here) to 33 or even 36 hours for Leaving Certificate candidates, with an average of 25-30 hours.

Primary school teachers work (in school) the same hours as their pupils, and sometimes longer where shift work operates owing to a shortage of teachers and/or classrooms. In Yugoslavia, therefore, they may have up to 36 hours a week. Secondary school masters and mistresses usually work rather shorter hours and in most countries have a guaranteed maximum, e.g. 24 hours in class where their pupils are in school for 30 hours. Near the top of a senior secondary school their teaching load may be 18 hours (France) or even 12 hours (Sweden) but they are expected to prepare lessons very thoroughly indeed and Swedish *lektors* are often engaged on research projects of their own, as are their university colleagues.

They have a qualification entitling them to teach in Universities or the senior forms of secondary schools or both. In some cases they alternate between school and university appointments, in others they combine them.

The teaching load of Secondary School staff in Britain is probably the highest in Europe—there is not much difference between Scotland and England in that respect. They normally have some free periods, but not as a matter of right: they are not entitled to additional payment (as on the Continent) if these free periods have to be sacrificed owing to a chronic staffing shortage or the temporary absence of one or more colleagues.

It is impossible to generalise about homework as the amount set varies from teacher to teacher and from school to school. Scotland differs from England and resembles the rest of Europe in that homework is usually set to primary school pupils, often at the "infant" stage. In senior secondary schools the load gradually increases from about $1\frac{1}{2}$ hours to 3 hours or more. But this is a heavier imposition in Scotland, where classes end at 4, and in France, where they end at 5, than in countries working the "extended morning".

Counting homework and classes together, Senior Secondary leavers in Scotland, as over most of Europe, work somewhat more than normal adult hours (though for 40 weeks, not 49 or 50 in the year) 45 hours are usual, 50 not exceptional. A German "Abiturient" and his Swedish counterpart may exceed 55 hours, but they are 19 whereas the Scottish Senior Leaver is usually 17, sometimes only 16. One may well ask whether, even in a 40-week year, these hours are not excessive, and whether they do not bring into operation the law of diminishing returns.

Jewish Education in Scotland

This appendix is mainly based on information and ideas supplied by the Rev. Dr. I. K. Cosgrove, J.P., the chief religious leader of the Jewish Community in Scotland, and Dr. E. Golombok, Editor of the Jewish Echo, Scotland's only Jewish newspaper.

The Jewish population of Scotland is approximately 16,000 souls—1500 in Edinburgh; 500 in Aberdeen, Dundee and smaller centres and 14,000 in Glasgow. There are slightly under 2,000 Jewish children attending schools throughout Scotland.

At present there are no Jewish schools in Scotland (in the sense of, say, Catholic schools, providing a full general education with a distinctive religious atmosphere). Jewish opinion is somewhat divided as to whether such schools should be set up. The main arguments against, which have up till now prevailed, are that Jewish parents and the synagogue community are together fully competent to bring up the children in the ancient faith, its majestic traditions and the whole ethical system that goes with them; while it is desirable that Jewish children, who will have to live and work with Gentiles when they grow up, should become accustomed to their presence meantime.

The arguments in favour, which are gaining ground steadily, include the following: (i) Present arrangements, outlined below, compel Jewish children to attend two schools instead of one, losing free time to the possible detriment of their health; (ii) By receiving their general education in schools where it is normal, rather than more or less exceptional, to be Jewish, they will gain valuable "naturalness" and self-confidence and their subsequent relationships with Gentiles will be if anything easier. This seems to be borne out by the experience of boys educated at Carmel College, England's only Jewish "Public School". (iii)

The prevailing atmosphere of schools and of teen-age society today is so non-religious and so "non-ethical" that sensitive and easily-influenced pupils do not really stand a chance against it, and even if they do, it is not fair to expose them to it, forcing them to expend in sheer resistance energy and emotions for which a more profitable outlet could be found.

The Glasgow Board for Jewish Education comprising leading members of the community—laymen, teachers and Rabbis—are therefore negotiating the purchase of a building suitable for the setting up of a Primary School, to which a Secondary School may be added in due course. Giffnock and Newlands Hebrew Congregation (Giffnock, Glasgow) already have a Nursery School on their premises.

With regard to purely Jewish education, every Synagogue conducts religious classes, the whole being under the general direction of the Board. These classes are held on Sundays and in the evenings. In addition the Board organises some form of religious instruction during the school periods of religious instruction. These are usually supervised by Jewish teaching staff when available in the schools. There are 50 full-time Day School teachers of the Jewish Faith in Glasgow: they include a Headmaster and several principal and senior teachers: the fact that they profess the Jewish Faith does not appear to present any obstacle to their legitimate promotion. Purely religious teachers, who visit the schools by arrangement, include Dr. Cosgrove, several Rabbis, and some theological students. Queen's Park Secondary School has, for some years provided Hebrew instruction as one of the choices of language for the Leaving Certificate. Most of the pupils who offer this subject are Jews: a few will be Christians seriously considering the Ministry as a possible career.

The Sunday morning and weekday evening classes, which form the core of Jewish instruction, are held at the Central Talmud Torah Classes as well as at all the local Synagogues. The Jewish Education Board, in addition to the Central Classes, has under its auspices a Hebrew and Rabbinical College for more advanced pupils.

"The aim of Jewish Education is to transmit our heritage to the next generation, to teach Jewish children the ethical and religious ideals, and the observances and practices of their faith, and to see that they become self-respecting and loyal members not only of their own community but of the wider community."

These are the aims as stated by Dr. Cosgrove: by changing one word in two places they become equally applicable to Christian education and indeed to any education worthy of the name. The fact is, however, that even non-religious Jews are generally far more Jewish than the average run of Christians, whether Catholics or Protestants, are whatever they profess to be. In the case of those who practise regularly, even if they do not fulfil all the observances in every meticulous detail, the difference is greater still.

How and why this is so is difficult to explain to those who have only so much of the Jewish inheritance as is incidental to their more or less diluted brand of Christianity: but it is immediately apparent to those of us who have even the thinnest of personal roots in the parched soil of Judaea.

The simplest way to put it is that being a Jew is not only a matter of holding certain beliefs and practising certain rites which may take up five minutes a day and an hour once a week. It implies a national or supranational allegiance, a way of life, the status of a pioneer in one country and of a semi-exile in all the rest, and the reverent yet familiar knowledge of what is probably the oldest language in the world and certainly much older than anything now spoken as a *national* language in Europe. Jews in the Yemen, Algeria, Canada and Russia, to mention but a few of the lands where they may be found, have much more in common than Catholics in equally diverse and scattered countries.

Furthermore Jewish status is by Jewish law heritable in the female line. A Jewess's children are all Jews, and so are all her daughter's children: but if her son marries a Gentile woman all his children are automatically lost to Judaism even though he may bring them up in the Faith and all its observances. The only way they can become Jews is to undergo the process of " conversion " which has extremely stringent requirements—the religious knowledge required, for instance, is not much less than that expected of an aspiring Rabbi. Christian status, however, is not heritable in itself, but is instantly and effortlessly conferred by the Sacrament of Baptism, the neophyte being, in most cases, a few days or weeks old and totally unaware of what is going on. Confirmation and equivalent rites by which adolescents or adults become full members of a Christian community are, broadly speaking, on the same level as Bar-Mitzvah (though the standard of religious instruction demanded is probably not so high). They are not comparable to Jewish " conversion "—because the Christian Churches are (with a few exceptions) very willing to welcome new members, whereas the Jewish tradition is to accept only those who know exactly what they are doing and why they are doing it, and who are fully confident that they can keep it up. This was not always so: Judaism was a proselytising faith in the time of Christ and the earliest converts to Christianity were, for the most part, either recent converts to the Jewish Faith or, more frequently, "God-fearers" who attended the Synagogue without giving it their formal allegiance. The break between the two religions actually came over the issue of whether such people should first become Jews before they could be accepted as Christians, or whether they should be admitted directly through baptism.

This event, and the fall of Jerusalem a few years later, were followed by a " tightening-up " of the Jewish religion very similar to that of the Catholic religion at the Council of Trent, though the process took somewhat longer, and ever since then, Jews have been most anxious to discourage and prevent their children from inter-marriage with Gentiles and (in nearly all countries) from being drawn into contacts and friendships which could lead to marriage. In Scotland as elsewhere, they direct their children's social activities into Jewish youth clubs or the Jewish sections of inter-denominational bodies such as the Boy Scouts, Girls' Guides, Girls' Training Corps, etc.

The disintegrating forces at work in contemporary society are naturally felt within the Jewish community, but not nearly to the same extent as among nominal and even practising Christians. The traditional influences of the Jewish home and Jewish family life are still vital religious and educational factors to be reckoned with in the upbringing of Jewish children. The Rabbis refer to children as the builders and tell a beautiful legend that, before God entrusted the Bible to Israel at Sinai, He demanded guarantees of them, and the only guarantee He accepted was their children. The importance of the place of the child in the community stressed by Disraeli when he coined the phrase "The youth of a nation are the trustees of posterity" makes one feel that he knew this legend.

In Jewish life the teacher is traditionally held in high esteem and teaching is regarded as the most honoured and respected of callings; indeed the word " Rabbi " means " my teacher ", and the greatest Jew, Moses, is called " Moses, our teacher ".

ISLE OF MAN

Educational Arrangements

(1) Education comes under a *Board of Tynwald* composed at present of five members of the House of Keys, who act as the Ministry of Education, and a mainly elected *Education Authority* who act as the County Education Committee, the Island being at the same time a "country" and a "county".

(2) *The Education Authority* consists of 24 persons directly elected by the adult population of the Island and 5 nominated by the *Board*. Some members of the Education Authority also happen to be in Tynwald but you cannot be a member of the *Authority* and the *Board* at the same time, nor can a teacher employed by the Authority be elected to it, though he may be elected to Tynwald.

(3) The 29 members of the Authority include at the time of writing a lawyer, 3 insurance agents, 6 former headmasters, 4 other former teachers, one of them a retired training college lecturer, two clergymen, a company director, an ex-superintendent of police, a farmer, a rich widow and a few landladies. Only four of them did not have a grammar school education or its equivalent (e.g. at King William's, the Island's only Public School).

(4) The members of the Authority have educated or are educating their children as follows: —

Twelve at schools run by the Authority.

Six at King William's or a similar but smaller girls' school —some of these probably attended local primary schools before going there.

One has a son at K.W's and a daughter in an authority school (or it may be the other way round).

One at a school in England.

Nine have no children.

(5) Points of comparison with British Authorities.

(a) All members are elected or nominated solely to deal with education. The elected members of County Education Committees are elected for all the purposes of local government and may have no particular interest in education, but they are reinforced by co-opted members with a more definite interest.

(b) The proportion of *adequately educated* members is much higher than in *Labour* authorities in Britain.

(c) The proportion of members with *teaching experience* (10 out of 29) is probably much higher than anywhere in Britain. This is because the Authority deals with Education and nothing else.

(d) The proportion of members with local school connections as former pupils or through sending their children to ordinary schools, is probably much higher than in most *Conservative* authorities in Britain.

(6) *How schools function.*

PRIMARY as in England but most of the country schools are one-teacher or two-teacher.

ELEVEN-PLUS EXAM nearly as in England, but for placing purposes only since the Secondary Schools are Comprehensive.

Secondary Boys' Comprehensive in Douglas

Girls' ,, ,, ,,

Mixed Comprehensives in Castletown, Peel and Ramsey.

These schools have a grammar side as in England and secondary modern streams with a variety of courses also as in England. In between is a semi-grammar stream in which pupils learn a language and also get some technical education. This corresponds to the curriculum of a Mittelschule (Middle School) in Germany. There is nothing quite like it in England.

G.C.E. (Northern Univs.) taken as in England.

Students from the Island often go to Sheffield, also to other Northern Univs. From King William's also to Oxford, Cambridge and Scottish Universities.

(7) *King William's.* Runs like an English Public School. But boys born or living on the Island benefit from a *Manx Reduction* of £30 a year (i.e. their fees are £330 instead of £360 —*per annum*) and the Manx Government makes up the £30 to the school out of public funds.

A similar system operates for the girls' school, *Buchan High.* Both are in Castletown.

(8) The Education Authority has two offshoots, the Children's Committee and the Welfare Committee. The latter handles Youth Clubs, camps coming to the Island and so on. These committees include some outside people co-opted only for that work.

(9) There is some risk that the Education Authority may disappear, it being felt that it is rather superfluous to have a *Board* and an *Authority* for an island with only 50,000 people. But it is doing good work at the moment, and is generally liked.

(10) *Further details* from:
  Director of Education (H. C. Wilkinson Esq., M.A.)
  Education Offices, Strand Street, Douglas, I.O.M.

The Educational System of Iceland
(By kind permission of the Editor of School and College)

The physical obstacles to education in Iceland are not unlike those encountered in the Highlands and Islands, only more severe. The national tradition, again, is very favourable to learning. Iceland is poorer than Scotland as regards material resources but no longer suffers from the grave handicap of being adjacent to a more prosperous country, attracting the ablest and most determined of her people and keeping her under permanent tutelage. Denmark was always much further away from Iceland than England from ourselves: Iceland's Parliament, the Althing, was never extinguished, and the nation recovered full independence in 1944.

In the circumstances I felt that a brief account of Education in Iceland would not be altogether out of place and have accordingly reproduced, with the Editor's kind permission, an article of mine published in the December 1961 issue of " School and College ".

Most people do not think of Iceland as part of Europe but as a country entirely separate. It nevertheless figures on all reputable maps of Europe, belongs to the Strasburg organisation and has now applied to join the Common Market. It is unique in several ways. Larger than the whole of Scotland, it has fewer inhabitants than Aberdeen. The language has not substantially altered for a thousand years. Any child of twelve can read the Eddas, contemporary not with Shakespeare, nor even Chaucer but with the Crusades, without the help of a dictionary. Icelanders have no surnames, only forenames and patronymics. Thus my Icelandic name would be Anton Cyrilsson and my son's, Andreas Antonisson — my wife remaining Jakobina Tomasdottir to the end of her days, since women are in no sense their husband's property. Furthermore anyone who wanted to find us in the telephone book would start by looking up our forenames.

Icelandic society has been up till now virtually classless, or as near it as you can get. A fisherman's three sons may become a doctor, a ship's captain and a builder's labourer repectively, and one of the doctor's sons may very well be a fisherman again. Nobody would think the worse of it, and he might well make a lot more money than his father.

Education has only been compulsory since 1906 but was widespread long before: the wandering poet of the twelfth century was closely followed by the wandering teacher of the thirteenth. Literacy was not rare among farmers and fishermen (between them nearly the whole population) *before* the Reformation, and was fairly general by 1800, though within a narrow compass: the Bible and the two Eddas were to be found in nearly every home, but as a rule little else. A majority of country children still come to school able to read and write. In principle, compulsory schooling begins at seven, lasting to fifteen, but home teaching is allowed up to the age of nine or ten, and encouraged in areas where it would be impossible to set up a regular day school.

The Minister of Education is ultimately responsible for all education, but municipal authorities manage primary and junior secondary schools (see below). The Catholic Church runs a primary school in Reykjavik, with antiquated facilities but a solid reputation; only 40 of the 170 pupils are Catholics. Its two other schools have been closed down, due to the State's refusal to subsidise them in any way. There is also an experimental independent primary school, again in Reykjavik. Pupils are admitted at the age of six but parents must sign an undertaking not to teach or attempt to teach them reading and writing before they are admitted.

A slowly decreasing number of itinerant teachers, dedicated but in general unqualified, operate in the North and East after the manner of their medieval forefathers, but sometimes with a jeep instead of a pair of skis. They remain a week or a fortnight at each of three or four farms, teaching all those children who live or can be gathered there, and then set homework to last a month or more.

In general they are being replaced by a combination of home tuition to the age of nine and boarding schools thereafter

—pupils normally staying for alternate fortnights and returning home with a load of "prep" to be done under their parents' supervision. This has been found more effective than tuition by wandering dominies, and *as effective* except as regards music and arts and crafts, as conventional education in a day school with a normal time-table. (Some use is also being made of school transport but far less than here, owing to the climate and roads).

Municipalities pay the teachers in these schools (as in regular day schools) but recover most of their outlay from the State, which also pays the housemothers' salaries. Overheads are met mainly by the municipalities, again as in the day-schools. Parents pay for their children's food or supply it in kind at market prices. Thus one farmer may pay his children's boarding fees in potatoes, another in milk or smoked ham.

The primary school course lasts six years from the age of seven. The Junior Secondary course lasts either for two years— the compulsory minimum—three or four years; the four-year schools have two streams, academic and practical. The others have a mainly academic curriculum which all follow as best they can.

A transfer exam, similar to our "Qualifying" but without intelligence tests, is taken by pupils at the end of the primary school course, and therefore at the age of twelve or thirteen (pupils normally enter the primary school in September or October of the year in which they reach the age of seven, but may be admitted earlier if they are bright enough and there is room for them). This examination is of some importance where the junior secondary school is streamed, but the Great Divide comes at 15/16 with the State Examination taken after three years in the junior secondary school. It may be regarded as rather harder than Common Entrance (though with two living languages—Danish and English—instead of Latin and French) and rather easier than "O" Level and the new Scottish Ordinary Grade. It is the sole qualification for entry to the three Grammar Schools, the Commercial School and the Teacher Training School—all with a four-year curriculum but the last-named not regularly giving access to the University. These five schools are directly subject to the Ministry of Education.

Of the three Grammar Schools Reykjavik is a day school but many country pupils live with relations or in lodgings, Akureyri, in Iceland's second town, is a boarding and day school with a majority of boarders, while Laugavatn is entirely a boarding school, with a separate boarding Junior Secondary School nearby. The Headmaster of Laugavatn Grammar School was until recently Professor of Icelandic at Cornell University, New York State; he and his charming American wife were so hospitable that I never got round to visiting the school, which was not functioning at the time anyway.

The curriculum of the three Grammar Schools is strictly regulated by the Ministry, and identical, to make life easier for pupils who move—not an infrequent occurence, since those who have to repeat a year prefer to do so elsewhere.

The first year's curriculum is in each case undifferentiated, while in the second, third and fourth years they are divided into a Languages "line" and a Maths/Science line. All however take some Science to the end, as well as Icelandic, a modern language, Physical Education and singing. In the second and third years all take *three* languages, English, French and German, but only French survives for Maths/Science finalists, while Danish is assumed to be known by the end of the second year.

The wastage is fairly high in the first and second years, decreases in the third and nearly disappears in the fourth when the Student Examination is taken.

All Icelandic schools are co-educational except a few with a very specialised curriculum (e.g. the Homecraft School at Laugavatn). Furthermore the boarding houses at Akureyri are mixed; at Laugavatn Grammar School there is one building but an iron curtain (literally) comes down at 10 p.m.; attempts to breach it directly or circumvent it by window-hopping are punishable by immediate expulsion, since parents expect the Headmaster to maintain stricter discipline than they would be able or willing to maintain themselves. In Reykjavik there is nothing to stop senior boys and girls from sharing a furnished flat somewhere in the town and some probably do: in the four months of summer holidays they can make enough on farms and trawlers or in the hotel and building trades to support themselves through the year, and 85% of the Laugavatn pupils actually *are* self-supporting.

Indeed one reason why Junior Secondary pupils try hard to get through the State Exam is that they are longing for a chance to get away from their parents, live in Reykjavik lodgings or in a largely self-governing teenage community at the boarding schools, and enjoy the semi-student way of life; while sometimes their parents don't mind being free of them awhile. Iceland's highly seasonal economy not merely permits but actively encourages such arrangements.

What of "accidents" whether in the boarding schools or elsewhere? The answer is simply that Iceland is geared to these accidents and takes them in her stride as she has done from Viking times. The illegitimacy rate is so high—26%—that it hardly matters whether a child is born in or out of wedlock, especially as, in the latter event, the parents usually marry in due course.

So far as the school is concerned, all that happens is that the girl will stay away as long as is medically necessary and will then continue her education, leaving the child with her parents; if it is obliging enough to appear in July or early August there may be no interruption at all (the secondary school year runs from 1st October to 31st May approximately).

So far as the child is concerned it will take its father's name if known, otherwise the maternal grandfather's. The known father or possible fathers singly or jointly maintain the child, with help from their parents if need be: if he/they cannot manage the girl's parents do what they can, thankful that another girl's parents will oblige in like manner if they have a son and he is involved in a similar "accident".

By way of compensation there is practically no juvenile delinquency or unnatural vice, and in the circumstances the *sum total* of moral problems to be faced by parents and by those acting *in loco parentis* is no greater than elsewhere.

Teachers in primary schools are trained in the teacher training school above, and are thereby qualified to teach in *two-year* Junior Secondary Schools also. Most Junior Secondary school staff are now graduates who have taken a three-year B.A. course *including education* but otherwise very similar to our Ordinary M.A. course. Masters and mistresses in Senior Secondary Schools have taken a four-year degree corresponding to the Swedish *Fil.Kand* or the Norwegian *Cand.Mag.* and roughly equivalent to the Scottish M.A. (Hons.). It is usually taken outwith Iceland, wholly or in part, since most school subjects cannot be studied to that level in Reykjavik's "pocket university" (800 students approximately; for details see *Universities of Europe*, end of Chapter I). Again they must have studied education in or after their degree course.

The three main educational problems to be resolved in Iceland are not unknown elsewhere. They are: —

(1) *Adjustment to a higher standard of living*, which has risen very fast indeed over the past twenty years, from being nearly as low as Spain's to being nearly as high as Sweden's. More "character formation" and "education for leisure", hitherto left to the parents and the local community, may now be required.

(2) *Adjustment to a high leaving age.* As in Scotland the system was devised to instil basic literacy, numeracy and godliness in all and to get the "lad o' pairts" to and through University. What is one now going to do with the older non-academic pupil? There is obviously scope for much more in the way of technical education.

(3) *Adjustment to a lack of solid motivation.* A great many pupils want to enter the Grammar Schools, as much to enjoy the way of life as for any truly academic reason. Having gained entry the bad ones (intellectually) exert a strong pull over the good but less ambitious ones, especially as there is no shortage of jobs and one can make as much in occupations which do not presuppose a degree or at any rate a Student-Examen as in those which do. The State Exam is another matter and those without it are at an increasingly serious disadvantage.

A further problem, particular to Iceland in its present form, is the appearance of a working class with a distinctive "non-culture". This could very well destroy the semi-Utopian atmosphere which the country has enjoyed hitherto, despite the deep depressions perenially centred over its lava-strewn moors.

Those in authority are giving much thought to all these problems and especially the last, which is not a matter of adjustment but of deliberate reversal. What has to be done, while the general drift of public opinion is still in favour of the classless society, is to prevent people who have "working-class" jobs from developing the mentality and way of life that go with them. Switzerland has succeeded up till now, but only because all Swiss workers are skilled and served by Italian labour, which is itself transitory and so does not create a minority problem.

It will be interesting to see how the Icelanders make out.

Toothill Committee's Recommendations on Education and Training

The Report of the Toothill Committee of Inquiry into the Scottish Economy was published on November 22nd, 1961, after two years of investigation. Its recommendations are given below, in so far as they are relevant to the problems of Scottish Education.

It should be borne in mind that the chairman of the committee was a businessman, as were six of its seven members: the seventh, Professor Wilson, is an economist. Their object was to find ways to make Scotland more prosperous, rather than ways to improve education, and their educational recommendations are largely conditioned by that purpose.

EDUCATION AND TRAINING

Education

33. Pupils in senior secondary schools should be able if they wish to specialise rather more in scientific and technical subjects; and university entrance requirements should be correspondingly adjusted.

34. Greater attention should be given to the development of more specialised studies in the sixth year.

35. An advanced grade of the Leaving Certificate as recommended by the Advisory Council on Education in Scotland should be introduced at an early date.

36. A stronger vocational bias should be introduced towards the end of the junior secondary courses.

37. Closer links should be established between the junior secondary schools and industry, commerce and technical colleges.

38. The technical education building programme should be speeded up and augmented.

39. Until the fundamental review of the apprenticeship system which we recommend (see 50) can take effect, it is necessary to obtain the maximum benefit from existing training methods. As soon as accommodation is available, day or block, release should be made compulsory.

40. Education authorities should be given a further opportunity to establish separate sub-committees with a substantial degree of delegated authority for the management of their technical colleges. Industrial members should be co-opted to these committees.

41. The planning of facilities for technical education cannot be undertaken properly until those concerned know what they have to prepare for. The Secretary of State should make an early declaration of intention on the points raised in the preceding paragraphs.

42. There should be a greater readiness on the part of the higher educational institutions to set up chairs in the newer technologies, and they should be able to create personal chairs. The procedure for setting up new chairs in Scotland should be reviewed.

43. Some courses in subjects relative to management should be included in the degrees for engineering and certain scientific disciplines and we would welcome an extension of the more specialised courses provided for managers by certain universities and central institutions. An early review should be carried out to determine whether the Royal College's residential centre for management studies is likely to be able to meet the full demands of industry and whether a similar centre should be established in the East of Scotland. Greater emphasis in the training of accountants should be placed on the various aspects of management work.

44. Urgent consideration should be given to the status of the major central institutions, particularly the Royal College of Science and Technology.

45. The shortage of specialised teachers in mathematics and science is likely to become even more serious unless the salaries for these teachers are brought more into line with those in industry: this would imply differences in pay according to subject within the teaching profession.

46. The attraction of firms from outside Scotland and the movement of labour would be facilitated if informal arrangements could be made which would offset the handicaps to which

a child from another area is subject in obtaining entrance to fee-paying schools. The Scottish Council should take this up and should also consider with the Government Departments concerned the provision for industrialists and others of information about schools.

Training

47. We attach great importance to the supply of skilled labour especially in certain key engineering trades. Shortages in these have already inhibited expansion and are likely to do so increasingly.

48. The Ministry of Labour should supplement the training by industry of men in these skills to the extent necessary to supply incoming industry, if necessary in co-operation with firms which have specialised experience of the kind required. Allowances under the Local Employment Act to incoming firms specifically for training could also help. Industry should continue to expand its own training.

49. Industry generally should be alive to the danger of expansion being hampered by shortages in skilled trades, which are likely to increase as the pace of the economy quickens. Both sides of industry should take immediate steps to meet shortages, for example, by asking the Ministry of Labour to help through their training courses. The Ministry of Labour's vocational training schemes should in consultation with industry be extended by increasing the number of occupations for which training is given and by widening the categories eligible for training.

50. The longer term needs of the economy require basic reforms. Over the whole of industry there is an urgent need for a fundamental review of the apprenticeship system to bring it into line with modern industrial methods. This should cover differentiation between skills and inter-changeability between trades, methods and duration of training, and the proper integration of technical education into the training system. Industries should undertake these reviews on their own initiative but if necessary the Ministry of Labour should take the lead. Priority might be given to the engineering, shipbuilding and building industries.

MANAGEMENT

66. As Britain is likely to face more intense competition, whether or not she joins the Common Market, Scottish manage-

ment should seek by every means to improve efficiency both in production and selling.

67. Management must place a greater reliance on science, for two broad reasons. The first is for fostering diversification in the economy; the second is for securing the benefits to the traditional industries from the greater application of science in the design and manufacture of products. Scientists and technologists should function not merely as specialists but should be fully introduced into the operational system of firms.

68. More attention will have to be paid in future to educational qualifications in recruiting management.

Comments by A. J. C. Kerr.

I am in entire agreement with most of these recommendations, arrived at by people far better qualified than myself. The only important exception is No. 45. Means must certainly be found of attracting Maths/Science teachers to the schools, but an increment for teaching these rather than other subjects would be inadmissible and unjustifiable.

To my mind there are only five valid grounds for differentials and increments, viz: —

    (i) higher qualifications,

    (ii) seniority,

    (iii) responsibility (including sole charge).

    (iv) efficiency, if an acceptable way of assessing it can be established,

    (v) " remote area " and the like.

The difference between *academic subjects*, which require a degree and from S.IV upwards an honours degree, and *non-academic subjects* which do not require one, is well established and generally accepted. But it would be highly invidious to set up any differences between the various academic subjects, whether on the score of their value to the community or on any other.

To be of any use whatever, the Maths/Science differential would have to be fairly massive, especially at the upper end of the incremental scale. Assuming Chapter V " Arts " teachers to be on a £800-£1600 scale, their Maths/Science colleagues would have to rise from £880 to £2400. This would be quite unacceptable to the profession as a whole. It would give rise to counter-claims by teachers of other subjects. Thus teachers of English could reasonably contend that, since their subject is essential, in this country, to the study of all others, it is the most important of all and they should accordingly enjoy the highest salaries. There would be disputes between historians and geographers as to the relative importance of their subjects. Domestic science teachers might demand to be paid more than teachers of Art or Music on the ground that what they teach is essential to civilized life while the other two subjects merely add to its enjoyment. I see no end to possible discord once this particular apple is thrown into one Common Room.

Other means must be found. I have incidentally suggested two of them in Chapter VII.

(a) Introduction of a higher degree corresponding to the Swedish *lektorat*. Its holders would be placed on a salary scale about 25% above that of Honours graduates. It would be open to education authorities to offer relatively more Maths/Science posts than "Arts" posts to *lektors* following in this the principle of the competitive *agrégation* in France. As in Sweden the teaching load of *lektors* would be relatively light, and they might therefore have research projects commissioned to them by industrial firms.

(b) Degrees "including education" for students who are prepared to teach but reluctant to commit themselves to a lifetime career in teaching. Ordinary degrees of this type would require a three-year course (not three years *plus* one year as for the present "Article 39" qualification). Honours degrees of this type would require four years, (not four years plus two terms as for the present "Chapter V" qualification).

Students taking these courses would receive grants higher than those given to other students, in return for an undertaking to teach for a period of years equal to the length of their course. This is already done in France. They would thus be able to enjoy their three or four years at a university rather more than they would have done otherwise.

After three or four years, as the case might be, their provisional teaching qualification would expire and it would then be open to them to take more profitable jobs in commerce or industry—or in any other walk of life, having given valuable service to education meantime. They could also take a brief but full-time "education" course lasting a term or two while drawing their full salary. This would put them on the "Article 39" scale with three increments or on the "Chapter V" scale with four increments depending on the quality of their degree.

At this stage it might also be possible for Ordinary graduates to return to University, do an "Honours" year followed by a term or two of "education" and be placed in the third incremental year of the "Chapter V" scale.

I think it would be found that many teachers, having entered the profession in this way, would choose to remain in it.

As regards Recommendation 66, I should like to stress the great importance of teaching languages *more effectively* and if possible *in greater number*. Germans, Frenchmen and Swedes of the executive class generally have English and often very good English. But they are favourably impressed by people who make some intelligent effort to address them in their own language, and making a favourable personal impression is a vital part of selling.

APPENDIX H

*The Advisory Council Report on Transfer from Primary
to Secondary Education*

As this book was going to press, the Scottish Education
Department published the Report of a Special Committee of the
Advisory Council, on transfer from Primary to Secondary Educa-
tion. This important and interesting document is available from
Her Majesty's Stationery Office, and no one seriously concerned
with Scottish Education should fail to obtain it.

The Report opens with a Historical Introduction and a
statement of present-day selection procedures, which it then
discusses in some detail. From the discussion there emerge five
significant facts:

(i) There is less general dissatisfaction regarding these
procedures than in England, because they are fairer in themselves
(less depends upon a child's physical and emotional state on one
particular day) and partly because a far larger proportion of
pupils are admitted to the Scottish equivalent of a Grammar
School in England.

(ii) Nevertheless these procedures are not fully satisfactory.
The scales are weighed in favour of pupils with a good cultural
background and those whose class teachers have not encountered
any pupils of really high ability. For these reasons objective
external tests are necessary, and scaling of teachers' estimates
highly desirable.

(iii) Transfer arrangements work better where teachers have
confidence in them and pass on this confidence to the parents.
The latter, especially, know too little about these arrangements
and the various types of course open to their children. This is
one of the main reasons for their insistence on an "academic"
and preferably a "two-language" course regardless of its suit-

ability for their children, or conversely of their children's suitability for such a course.

(iv) No useful purpose is served by retaining less able pupils in primary schools or departments beyond the normal age for transfer, unless their progress has been seriously retarded through prolonged illness for instance.

(v) The number of pupils whose parents appeal to transfer boards and eventually to the Secretary of State has shown a considerable increase since existing procedures were established. There has also been a large increase in the number of pupils transferred from "non-academic" to "academic" schools or courses.

The Special Committee have made many recommendations which I have not given here, as I think anybody who reads "Schools of Scotland" should also buy their Report, drawn up by people in every way more highly qualified than myself. Several of them happen to coincide with mine: thus they have recommended greater attention to "very able pupils and the best of the able", closer liaison between primary and secondary schools or departments, "a searching survey of the primary school curriculum" and greater use of "setting" in Secondary Schools. They have also recommended greater attention to pupils at "the lower end of the intellectual scale" and have urged teachers and education authorities concerned with junior secondary schools (and presumably with "non-academic" classes in "omnibus" schools) to be "much more adventurous in adapting the work of such schools to the non-academic child".

In my opinion the Report is not only important and interesting but very well-thought-out. My only regret is that the Special Committee did not consider more fully the transfer procedures and the primary and secondary curricula of certain other countries, from which we may have a great deal to learn.

Thus, as I have indicated elsewhere, East Germany has special primary classes for pupils of exceptional ability, with a "primary" atmosphere suitable for their age, but an enriched curriculum which includes Russian and General Science, and some initial contact with specialists in these subjects. Several of the West German Länder have a selection procedure which, after a preliminary "weeding-out" consists essentially of trial classes in a Gymnasium (Senior Secondary School) jointly conducted by primary school teachers and Gymnasium masters and mistresses. Only the better 50% of the transfer age group normally get as far as these trial classes, but *any* parent, where they exist, is entitled to demand that his child be given a chance to take part, and this is the German equivalent of our "appeal" procedure.[1]

It might also have been worthwhile considering the introduction of a language into the "non-academic" curriculum for all except those at "the lower end of the intellectual scale". This is generally done in Scandinavia and tends to appease the parents of the pupils thus initiated to English: I am not aware that the Swedish spoken in working-class districts of Stockholm, or the Norwegian and Danish spoken in the corresponding parts of Oslo and Copenhagen, is appreciably worse than the English normally spoken by our 15-year-old leavers. I remain strongly of the opinion that we should experiment with "non-academic" language teaching on a far larger scale than at present, and probably with languages other than French. This would involve sending out many of our existing teachers and students on a succession of holiday courses in the countries in which these languages are spoken—not at all a bad thing in itself since there are many minds that need to be enlarged and many prejudices crying out to be dissolved.

After the rest of this book had been completed, and too late for me to make any substantial changes, a reply to parts of my questionnaire arrived from Mrs. C. McFadden, a teacher at Castlebay Primary School and a member of Inverness-shire County Council (though not of its Education Committee, since she is a serving teacher). "The manner in which Education Committee members are appointed is far from satisfactory, except to themselves. Little disadvantage arises nowadays from the sparse population and remoteness of the islands (educationally speaking).

"The main purpose of Scottish Education is to produce basically good Christian citizens. The Scottish system might tend to produce someone who is middle-class generally, but not an unskilled labourer—who is more a product of circumstances. The ideal of liberal education is ever "young" and desirable and cannot be excessive, irrespective of changing circumstances

---

[1] The selection procedure also admits pupils to the *Mittelschule* or *Realschule*, whose curriculum leads up to the equivalent of our "Ordinary Grade", or English "Ordinary Level". With the Middle School Certificate they may subsequently join the senior forms of a Gymnasium, where they will be placed in a "Non-Latin" stream.

and contemporary society needs. Nor does it arise from nor account for the considerable degree of emigration and unemployment in Scotland.

"English schools do not produce more 'leaders' than Scottish schools. An English 'leader' would need to be an individual responsible and independent as much as a Scotchman (Mrs. McFadden's spelling, not mine!) Scotch 'individuals' are at their best in hierarchical position, responsible and independent as much — if not more so — as Scottish doctors, engineers and lawyers.

"On the whole there is little difference in the attitude to Education of Conservative, Liberal/Independent and Labour authorities: any difference may be in the attitude of different classes, prosperous and non-prosperous, professional and manual. There is no difference in the attitude to Education of *Authorities* in rural and industrial areas, and there is no difference in the attitude to Education of Catholic and Protestant schools.[1] There often is a difference in attitude to Education among the inhabitants of rural and industrial areas.

"Pupils from rural schools tend to be more ambitious than those from the towns. Grant-aided schools serve the greatest needs, work hardest and produce the backbone of the country. Boarding schools seem to serve easy-going "collar & tie" section, concentrating more on culture and art (On my knowledge of Fettes, Loretto, Glenalmond, Gordonstoun, Fort Augustus and Rannoch I cannot agree with this).

"There is no case for earlier transfer of able pupils to secondary schools, or the teaching of some secondary subjects in Primary VII or for the setting up of "A-plus" streams.

Sufficient account has been taken of the fact that our children are maturing earlier. There would be a case for Sixth Form Work at the top of our Senior Secondary Schools, this to link up with University reform.

"As a rule the sort of people who become teachers are hard-working men and women from the working classes (in which I take it Mrs. McFadden includes the crofting community, which I include with the lower middle-class because they are self-employed). More come from industrial areas like North-East

---

[1] As explained elsewhere Castlebay School is not a Catholic School in the same sense as those in Glasgow and Edinburgh for instance. It is *the* local school in which over 90 per cent of the pupils happen to be Catholics, while special arrangements are made for the Protestant minority.

than from farming South (I never knew the North-East was "industrial" in the commonly accepted sense).

"The young people who come out of our schools are healthy, self-possessed, independent, smart and knowledgeable, tending to be rather ungrateful and selfish.

"Our Educational System is near enough satisfactory mean-time but Education Committees should be replaced by *ad hoc* elected Education Authorities as in Scotland 1918-29. Teachers should be eligible. The Western Isles should *not* form a separate Educational Area. Leave well alone: this is not a new idea, it was examined some twelve years ago.

"There should be no lengthening of the Secondary School day, but a term to a year in a boarding establishment at the end of the course could be worthwhile — some adventure training would be useful.

(Are salaries too high for the minority of teachers who tag along doing as little as they can get away with, etc,?) "Non-sense! It's more of those teachers we need, to lay down good foundations and get children to develop early some initiative, not spoonfeed them all the time. In primary schools there is often too much actual teaching, too little practice by the pupil. Supervised written exercises are valuable."

My comments and queries are given in brackets above. I should add that Mrs. McFadden's views constitute very much of a minority report on several important points, among them the arrangements which might or should be made for pupils of considerably more than average ability. The consensus of opinion in favour of *ad hoc* authorities, to which she adds her weight, is quite crushing. Only three people among all those I consulted were prepared to defend education committees as at present organised, and of those three only one had ever taught, and only those three considered that teachers should be excluded from them. Lord Lothian supported reformed education committees, with representatives of parents and teachers elected as such— everyone else was in favour of *ad hoc* authorities apart from a few who advocated more thoroughgoing centralisation with considerable powers in the hands of a Teachers' Council.

Few would agree with her apparent support for the recruit-ment of more "minimum-effort" teachers.

Edinburgh's Independent Schools

(By the Head Master of George Heriot's School, Edinburgh,
reprinted by kind permission of the Editor of *The Scotsman*.)

Among the features which lend distinction to the city of
Edinburgh, the number and quality of its educational institutions
ranks high; and among these the endowed and independent
schools hold an honoured place. The expression "fee-paying,"
so often used to identify them, is convenient; but it carries
irrelevant emotional undertones, and it tells nothing of their
differing but colourful histories, of their essential character, or
of the notable contribution they have made to educational
development in Scotland. The story of the older of these schools
falls into two distinct parts—from their early foundation until
1869, and again from that date up to the present time.

The origins of the Royal High School lie farthest back in
time; written evidence of its existence first appears in the City
Archives under the date 1497. The erection of a new High School
in the garden of Blackfriars Monastery is recorded for 1578. Two
hundred years later another new building in turn was erected to
accommodate the School; to-day that building is still to be seen
at the foot of Infirmary Street, and houses the Natural Philosophy
department of the University.

The High School finally moved in 1829 from Old Edinburgh
to the New Town, there to occupy the impressive present building
on the Calton Hill.

Until the early seventeenth century the High School had
remained the only institution of its kind in the city. In 1628,
however, the foundation stone was laid of the first of the great
Scottish charitable endowments, George Heriot's Hospital.

Heriot's example was presently to inspire imitation. At a
meeting of the Merchant Company of Edinburgh on June 4 1694

the Master made the announcement that " Mary Erskine, relict of James Hair, druggist, had mortified Ten Thousand Merks for the maintenance of Burges children of the female sex "; and in 1706 Mary Erskine herself spent 12,000 on the purchase of a house " towards the use of a hospital to be called the Hospital of Mary Erskine ".

In his will George Watson, shrewd businessman and first accountant to the Bank of Scotland, had gifted " five thousand merks Scots " to Heriot's Hospital for the purpose of maintaining two foundationers there; and when he died in 1723 he left a very substantial sum " to raise a Hospital for entertaining and education of the male children and grandchildren of decayed merchants in Edinburgh ".

Then, on the death of James Gillespie, snuff merchant, in 1797, it was found that his bequests, destined mainly for the establishment of a hospital (home) for aged men and women, included a modest sum to build and conduct a " free " school for poor boys. Again, in 1822 the Society of Writers to the Signet, as trustees for the estate of John Watson, successfully petitioned Parliament for powers to establish and endow a hospital for the maintenance and education of fatherless children.

Finally (for this was to be the last occasion of the founding of a hospital school) on his death in 1814, Daniel Stewart, a member of the Scottish Court of Exchequer, left his fortune in the hands of trustees with an instruction that it should accumulate until it was sufficient to build and endow a hospital for boys. This purpose was achieved soon after the middle of the century. For 200 years therefore from 1659 charitable endowments grew steadily in number in the city of Edinburgh.

They grew no less steadily in influence, and by their pattern were destined to shape the educational development of the city and of the whole of Scotland. Heriot's Hospital, opened in 1659 in the building which it still occupies, soon housed 180 boys in residence.

The Merchant Maiden Hospital was founded next, in 1697 in a wing of the then Merchants' Hall in the Cowgate.

In 1818 the hospital moved to a new site in Lauriston, close to Heriot's; and in 1869 it removed again to the so-called Hopetoun Rooms, its present site at the west end of Queen Street, with the title the Edinburgh Ladies College. (In 1944, on the 250th anniversary of its foundation, the title was fittingly changed to the Mary Erskine School for Girls.).

Fully 40 years were to elapse after the foundation of the Merchant Maiden Hospital before the next endowment took concrete form. In 1738 Watson's Hospital Trust feued from the Heriot Trust $7\frac{1}{2}$ acres of ground at Lauriston, and on this site they erected George Watson's Hospital.

The free day school in which Gillespie had desired 100 poor boys between the ages of six and twelve to be taught reading, writing and arithmetic opened in 1803, in what is now Gillespie Crescent, with only 65 pupils on the roll, and with a single master.

The provision made in his will by Daniel Stewart for the endowment of a hospital for boys was finally translated into reality when his trustees completed in 1853, from the plans of David Rhind, the handsome building now known as Daniel Stewart's College.

Throughout this long period the Royal High School had continued to play its impressive and increasingly important part as the city's grammar school. It was no uncommon thing in these early days for able scholars from the hospital schools to transfer to the High School for a year or two before entering the University.

The growth of the New Town of Edinburgh, however, on the north side of the Nor' Loch had given rise to the demand for a new school to meet the needs of those resident in it. The High School "at the east side of the Kirk o' Field" was inconveniently situated for them. In October 1824 Edinburgh saw the doors opened of its second grammar school, The Edinburgh Academy.

If the eighteenth century had seen the full development of the hospital school system, the nineteenth brought a new phenomenon in the private owner. In 1827 Loretto opened as a private school, owned by the Rev. Thomas Langhorne, D.D.; October 1832 was the date of the opening of the Edinburgh Institution; and in 1833 Mr. Charles Chalmers came to reside in the old Merchiston Tower and set up a school under the name of Merchiston Castle Academy.

Education up to this point had centred almost exclusively on the two great classical languages and their literatures. In 1832 the then head master of George Watson's Hospital, the Rev. Robert Cunningham, A.M., resigned that office in order to open the "Edinburgh Institution of Languages, Mathematics, &c." Cunningham himself later wrote " In 1831 the idea struck me that there was room for an Institution in Edinburgh for combining with classics the teaching of modern languages, practical and theoretical mathematics and the elements of science more extensively than had hitherto been attempted." His prospectus showed that his curriculum (for boys of twelve to fifteen) had what would to-day be called a vocational bias.

Cunningham's pioneer work was one sign of dissatisfaction —dissatisfaction with the content of the curriculum. But signs were not lacking that the whole hospital system had ceased to command confidence.

Significantly, the trustees of Sir William Fettes, who died in 1836, took account of this trend in public opinion; and when Fettes College was opened in 1870, it did so in the new form of a boys' boarding-school, at which the majority should pay fees, and a minority, whose fees would be payed in full from the Founder's estate, should take their place on equal terms with them as "Foundationers" or (if they came from state-aided schools in Scotland) as "Foundation Scholars".

The pattern was clearly that of the English Public School, as the principal trustee, Lord Inglis, intended. The spirit of Arnold had reached Scotland.

It is to the credit of several of the endowments that their governing bodies had shown a practical awareness of the necessity for a bolder conception of their responsibilities. Thus, the governors of Heriot's, conscious of the city's need of more schools, had built in 1838 the first of what finally numbered seventeen Foundation or "Outdoor" schools at various points throughout Edinburgh.

Similarly, the Merchant Company as early as 1852 had obtained Parliamentary consent to admit day scholars to George Watson's Hospital and paying pupils to the Merchant Maiden. The classic report of Professor Simon Laurie in 1868 finally convinced the public that the hospital system had had its day; and the joint efforts of the Merchant Company and the Heriot Trust led to the passing of the Endowed Institutions (Scotland) Act in 1869, whereby the Governors of endowments were enabled readily to modify their endowment schemes.

The abandonment of the Hospital system had another, possibly unexpected, result: it seemed to bring about an upsurge of the progressive spirit. Significantly, the earliest examinations (1888-9) for Leaving Certificates were taken by a larger number of schools in Edinburgh than in any other Scottish town; when science first appeared as a Leaving Certificate subject in 1899, two of the eight schools presenting candidates were in Edinburgh —the Academy and Heriot's.

Indeed, the history of all the endowed schools in modern times may be said to begin anew at this point. Oddly enough, a decade before (in 1872) the Royal High School had passed under the control of the Town Council, and at once took on the character of a maintained school. Most of the endowed schools abandoned their residential character either immediately or within a short time.

Almost 200 boys in the Senior department of the Royal High School hold scholarships entitling them to free education. In Heriot's likewise, in the Senior School one boy in every four enjoys a similar privilege from the Founder's bounty. The Merchant Company maintain foundationers in each of their four schools. At Fettes one boy in sixteen is a foundationer or foundation scholar. John Watson's has both boy and girl foundationers.

The year 1869 was therefore, a milestone in the history of the endowed schools.

To-day the four Merchant Company schools house over 4300 pupils. Watson's Boys' College, spaciously accommodated at Colinton Road and Myreside, has a roll of over 1500; each of the other three schools has a roll slightly above 900. It is the intention of the Merchant Company Board to rebuild George Watson's Ladies' College and the Mary Erskine School more adequately, with playing-fields adjoining; a site for the latter school has already been acquired.

Heriot's ceased to be a hospital school in 1886, and, to meet the needs of a roll which rose rapidly from 180 to over 1000 day boys by the turn of the century, embarked on an elaborate building programme on the periphery of the school grounds.

Provision for a Preparatory Department was made in 1932 (until that time boys were not admitted before the age of seven): to-day the school houses over 1500 boys in the age range 5-19.

Gillespie's School had been meagrely endowed—prior claim on the endowment lay with the provision of a Home for old men and women. In 1908 the Merchant Company, facing the fact that the endowment was inadequate to meet necessary expansion, transferred the school to the then School Board. The school moved in 1914 to the present building in Warrender Park Crescent, and in 1924 it developed a post-intermediate department.

The number of boys enrolled gradually diminished; and by the early 1930s the school had acquired its present distinguished status as James Gillespie's High School for Girls. The present building and site are no longer adequate for this large, progressive school, and plans are well advanced for new modern buildings nearby.

John Watson's had opened its doors on its pleasant site above the Dean Village on August 12, 1828, with a roll of 50 children. For over a century it maintained its fine charitable character, making striking advance during the distinguished headmastership of Mr. George Rowe. In 1934 it widened its scheme to admit pupils other than foundationers.

The " Institution " continued to be run as a privately owned school until 1910, when it was taken over by a company formed by former pupils. In that same year the headmastership passed to Mr. Walter Hardie, to whom the school was to owe much.

Under his wise guidance it found its modern home in Melville Street in 1920, a move which was later to give it its new name of Melville College. Recent expansion has raised the roll to nearly 500; and the status of the college is now that of a grant-aided school.

The number of boys attending the Edinburgh Academy in 1928 reached 521; to-day it falls just short of 1000. The several boarding-houses accommodate about 120 boarders. The Academy in modern times owes its essential character to Mr. R. J. Mackenzie, Rector from 1888 to 1901; and it has steadily maintained its reputation for progressive innovation.

Strong imprint

In 1862 Loretto had been taken over by Dr. Hely-Hutchinson Almond, who remained head for 41 years and left his strong imprint on the school. The school roll rose from slightly over 100 in his time to some 300 to-day, expansion being met by the acquisition in 1951 of the historic Pinkie House. On Almond's death in 1903 the school was taken over by a company formed by old Lorettonians; in 1945 it was transferred to the present trustees, who form the governing body.

Seventeen years before 1870, the momentous year in Scottish education, Merchiston Castle Academy was bought by Mr. John J. Rogerson, at that time one of the assistant masters. The 35 years of his headmastership are closely associated with the rise and development of the school to its full stature.

Two years before his retirement he arranged for the school to pass from his private ownership to that of a company, largely composed of Merchistonians. In 1924, pressure of numbers and of new projects compelled the directors to purchase the estate of Colinton House, where the school now is, with 275 boys in residence.

Fettes College, patterned deliberately on the English Public School, was opened in 1870 with 40 foundationers and 11 other boarders housed in the College or in what was to be the first of several boarding houses, Glencorse (the architect was David Bryce). The college made a most auspicious beginning under its first head master, Dr. A. W. Potts, and numbers rose quickly to 200 boys. Individual houses were added from time to time (the latest in 1951): the present numbers in the College are 450.

The pattern of educational provision within the schools this article has described is diverse but comprehensive; and the contribution of their products in every field of human endeavour, continues to be impressive.

The School Ship MS Dunera

One of the most interesting experiments in Scottish Education—though most of the young participants are in fact English—is the School Ship MS *Dunera*. The idea of a School Ship first occurred to Mr. Tam Dalyell (Dalyell of the Binns), a Cambridge Old Etonian teaching at Bo'ness Academy, while he was laid up following an accident. He developed this idea in his book, *The Case for Ship Schools*, published by the Civic Press, Glasgow, in 1960. This book fell into the hands of a Director of the British India Steamship Company who were at the time considering what to do with the troopship *Dunera*, whose services were no longer required by the Government. It was thus that the first School Ship serving the purposes of general education (there are training ships for Merchant Navy cadets, etc.) came into being: her cruises proved so popular that another troopship, the *Devonshire*, has now been converted into the School Ship *Devonia* and came into service just before this book was published.

Dunera's second cruise is described below by one of her passengers, Miss Lesley Clark, formerly a Latin/French pupil of mine at Jedburgh Grammar School, who is now at Hawick High School.

" At half past four in the afternoon of July 1st, 1961, to the strains of the bagpipes MS *Dunera*—12,615 gross tons and a former troopship—moved slowly away from Greenock to begin a fourteen day cruise, carrying schoolboys and girls from all over Scotland. This was the second trip that the ship would make under the heading of an " Educational Cruise " and this time she was calling at Corunna, Gibraltar and Lisbon.

As a young nurse led us down flights of iron steps and along twisting passages I felt quite sure I would never know my way about what was to my unaccustomed eyes a very large vessel. I was one of the Jedburgh and Melrose party which consisted of nine girls and four boys. With the other girls in my party I found myself in a long dormitory containing twenty exactly similar iron bunks, suspended by chains in double rows on two sides of the room. Beside each pair of beds was a wooden locker with plenty of hanging space as well as a room for folding clothing in. As there were twenty beds and only nine of us we were sharing with a girls' party from Girvan, the members of which were about the same age as we were, i.e. thirteen to fifteen. On this particular cruise, however, the majority of girls and boys were older than us, many being in their late 'teens. There was great rivalry over who should sleep in the top bunks and who in the bottom, the top being by far the most popular, and it was to our satisfaction that my friend Anne Robertson and I managed to bag adjoining bunks in the top row. Above my bunk there was a wooden speaker which, when we were busy cramming our luggage into the lockers, announced that the second sitting was to go to the canteen for the evening meal.

Since there were too many passengers to dine at once there were three sittings and we found that we were in the second. The food was served not on plates but on a tin tray divided into sections for each part of the meal. There was a long open hatch from which we collected what we wanted served by the friendly smiling Asians who made up most of the crew. The meals were very good, our only complaint being that sometimes it was impossible to finish eating in time because of the very generous helpings. We were rather surprised as we became accustomed to dining on the ship, to realise how varied and of what high quality the food was: it was not unusual to be served with such luxuries as chicken followed by ice cream.

Having finished dining the second sitting was summoned over the loudspeaker to the Assembly Hall. When after some difficulty we arrived there we were shown the correct way to make our bunks and warned that we would be responsible for the tidiness of our dormitory and were reminded that there would be a daily inspection of dormitories by the captain. After we left the hall we went up on deck and presently the green fields of Ireland came in sight. We were to pick up some fresh boys and girls who were coming on the cruise. As the boat bearing our new passengers approached many of us hung over the rails and took a long first real look at Ireland. When the ship moved on again cutting through the grey sea like a knife through butter, Anne and I wandered around the deck, looking with interest at the many things to which we were unaccustomed, before deciding to turn in, for although it was still early in the evening and the lights were not put out till ten o'clock, the excitement and new experiences of the day had left us exhausted.

The next few days were spent in finding the way about the ship and getting used to life on board ship. Each dormitory was named after some famous person and a badge with the name of the dormitory had to be worn all the time. The dormitory I was in was called Nelson and was one of the dormitories represented by the colour green. At our Muster Station all the names of the green dormitories were painted on the wall so that in the event of an emergency we should be able to find our proper places. (An emergency drill had taken place almost as soon as the ship left Greenock and we had been shown how to wear our life jackets, which we found to be extremely uncomfortable). Each party had its own classroom but as it was holiday time I do not think anyone did much in the way of the "three R's" and when told to go to our classrooms we usually spent our time listening to our party leader tell us about the places we should visit, and in asking questions about such things as foreign currency. Usually after half an hour in the classroom we took part in one of the organised deck games of which there were many, including deck hockey, deck cricket, quoits, deck tennis and medicine ball.

Apart from the organised games there was a great number of facilities laid on for our amusement. A salt water swimming pool was the scene of many water polo matches and duckings as well as being used for ordinary swimming. For those not interested in swimming there was a Games Room where one could play table tennis. The Recreation Room however was perhaps the place where most people liked to spend a lot of their leisure time. There one could play at one of the tables that were spread all over the room, such games as draughts, chess, monopoly, ludo and snakes and ladders, or read a book chosen from the library open to everyone. Here also one could buy lemonade, sweets, sun hats, sun oil and numerous other articles which would be useful when the days became very hot. A juke box was installed in one of the corners of the Recreation Room with many of the latest pop recordings.

Near the end of the cruise a concert was arranged which ran for two nights with considerable success, but when not making entertainment ourselves, the Assembly Hall was sometimes used to show films.

On the third day we reached Corunna, the first of our ports of call. Seething with excitement we could hardly wait to step on foreign soil, but even from the ship we could see the vast difference between this Spanish town and our home town. Eventually the loudspeaker announced that the Jedburgh and Melrose party was to disembark. That was the most wonderfully exciting day in my life. Our party leader, Mrs. Veitch, arranged that we might spend the morning by ourselves shopping, as long as we were with at least one other person.

In the afternoon we all piled into a coach and were driven through the streets of the town and then into the country. The first place the coach stopped was at a large shady garden in which was the tomb of Sir John Moore. We were then taken to other places of interest before going back to the ship which sailed at 8 o'clock. Before we sailed away from Corunna we were treated to a display of Spanish dancing which was performed to music of the Spanish bagpipes!

Two days later we had a glimpse of Africa on our way to Gibraltar. At Gibraltar the routine followed at Corunna was changed. In the morning we were driven by car to see some of the famous Rock sights. The first place to be visited was of course the home of the beloved apes, then we were driven up on the rock and shown the places the Queen had been when she had come to Gibraltar. We had been provided with packed lunches and after the car trip our afternoon was ours to spend as we pleased. That night a concert was put on by some of the Gibraltese and was performed in the Assembly Hall, and it was with real regret that we waved goodbye and sailed away.

Life on board was now even more enjoyable than before. Several more efforts were made to entertain us and work in the classroom was almost non-existent because by now all the schools back home were on holiday. At lunch times record requests were played over the loudspeakers and in the evenings dances took place on a deck gaily decorated for the occasion. A news sheet was brought out called the *Dunera News*.

It was a Sunday when we reached Lisbon, our last port of call. In the morning we were driven around the beautiful capital by coach stopping at such places of historical interest as the Royal Coach House and of architectural interest as the Geronimo Monastery. The afternoon was our own and since all the shops were closed Anne Robertson's sister Christine and myself decided to join up with the party of Govan girls who were going to Estoril, the place where so many exiled monarchs decide to spend their exile.

After Lisbon it was full speed ahead for home. Now that the cruise was approaching its end many competitions were arranged. There were to be prizes for essays on the cruise, making a speech about the places visited, a prize for the girls' dormitory which had earned most marks for tidiness and one for the boys. There were to be table tennis tournaments and competitions to find the best kept log books and diaries. There was also to be a Beauty Competition to find Miss Dunera and a competition to find Mr. Dunera. A few days before the end of the cruise a Prizegiving was held and the prizes awarded. On the second last day certificates and badges were issued to everyone as a memento of the holiday of a lifetime."

Note. MS Dunera has also cruised to the Norwegian fjords, Stockholm, Leningrad and Helsinki, Casablanca and many places in the Mediterranean. Med. cruises mainly take place in the autumn and winter, and pupils join at Marseilles, etc. by special trains. Such cruises cost about £50, including rail fare, for dormitory class passengers—i.e. pupils. Britain-to-Britain cruises, such as the one described above, may cost them £35 approx. These cruises, and the pupils' fares, are not subsidised in any way.

One party leader is carried free per 15 pupils. He/she need not be *their* teacher. Thus Mrs. Veitch, mentioned above, teaches in the primary department of Jedburgh Grammar School, whereas the Jedburgh pupils were all secondary.

Other adults may travel as cabin class passengers, their fares being approximately 50/- higher than those quoted above. Further details from the British India Steamship Co., 91 Bothwell Street, Glasgow, C.1.

Though in its present form the School Ship idea owes its inspiration to Tam Dalyell's book, a great deal of valuable pioneer work was accomplished between the two World Wars by Mr. John L. Kinloch, F.E.I.S., also in co-operation with the British India Steamship Company. An article by Mr. Kinloch, which appeared in *The Weekly Scotsman*, was seen by the same director who read "The Case for School Ships".

The main difference between Mr. Kinloch's inter-war scheme and the present one was that "Dilwara" was chartered by a committee of teachers whereas "Dunera" remains the full responsibility of the B.I. Company, who employ a Director of Studies and an Assistant Director of Studies as Ship's Educational Officers. Furthermore accommodation is booked directly from the Company, whereas under the old arrangement interested teachers applied to the chartering committee.

Another point is that Mr. Kinloch's purpose was and is essentially idealistic — the promotion of peace through international understanding among young people — Mr. Dalyell's purpose was and is essentially educational with the same sort of idealism, however, plainly visible at the back of his mind.

Mr. Kinloch, now well into his eighties, has meanwhile set up another organisation known as the British Peace Envoys. Details may be had from him at Lethington, Kilcreggan, Dunbartonshire. He hopes to charter "Dunera" in the summer of 1963 for a cruise visiting Scandinavia and the Soviet Union.

Further details contributed by the General Manager of the British India Steam Navigation Company Ltd.

1. The Ship's Company consists of nearly 300 Officers and Ratings and includes 2 Surgeons, 2 Nursing Sisters, 5 Matrons and 6 Masters-at-Arms, as well as a Director and a Deputy Director of Education. The Captain is entirely responsible for his ship and everything which happens on board. Apart from the Company's Regulations, his position of entire responsibility rests also under statutory powers given to him by the Merchant Shipping Acts. He maintains control through the Heads of the five Departments within the Ship, namely, Deck, Engine, Purser's, Medical and Education. The Director of Education is regarded as the Headmaster of the "boarding school" and maintains control of school activities through daily conferences with teachers in charge of groups of pupils and through his Daily Orders which allocate Lecture Rooms, other educational aids, deck facilities and recreational amenities to each group. The working day consists of six periods, three in the morning and three in the afternoon and evening activities, which commence at 7-30 p.m., are also arranged in this way.

2. Formal education consists of: (a) Lectures given by the Director of Education and his Deputy concerning the next places

to be visited during the cruise, supported by suitable educational films of the country concerned.

(b) The progress of study work in Lecture Rooms by each group of pupils under its own teacher. The subject of this Lecture Room work is entirely within the discretion of the teacher in charge.

3. "DUNERA" carried over ten thousand pupils during the first nine months of this unique form of educational travel and we are happy to report that no pupils were lost and that there were only three cases of illness which required early operative treatment. These were all cases of appendicitis and the operations were performed at the next port visited, the children being repatriated by air. All expenses were covered by the compulsory insurance, the cost being 5s. per head. Few disciplinary steps became necessary and the Director of Education, in conjunction with the Party Leaders concerned, was quite able to deal with the minor breaches which arose.

4. We understand that passage money is normally paid by parents and, so far as we know, there is no subsidy by the Scottish Education Department or benevolent organisations. Certain Local Educational Authorities grant some financial assistance for authorised school journeys and, we believe, they are prepared to regard "DUNERA" and "DEVONIA" in this light.

5. The extent to which pupils have benefited from travelling in "DUNERA" is a question which is best answered by experienced educationists and perhaps parents. We have had many hundreds of letters of appreciation from both categories and you may perhaps prefer to make further enquiries from those who can give you first-hand views.

Note The School Ship "DEVONIA" (formerly the troopship "DEVONSHIRE") entered service in April 1962 on a programme of cruises similar to those already being undertaken by "DUNERA". She is identical in all respects to "DUNERA".

THE REFORMERS' SCHEME FOR SCOTTISH EDUCATION, AS PROPOSED IN THE BOOK OF DISCIPLINE (1560)

Reproduced (with some additional explanations) by Kind permission of the "Clarendon Press," Oxford.

UNIVERSITY SPECIALIST COURSES

AGE	GRADUATE IN DIVINITY		GRADUATE IN MEDICINE		GRADUATE IN LAW
25					
24	2nd Class:	24	Medicine	24	2nd Class: Law
23	Divinity	23	at same	23	Municipal
22	New Testament	22	college	22	Roman
21	Old Testament	21	as	21	4 yrs.
20	5 yrs.	20	Arts	20	1st Class (1 yr.)
19	1st Class (1 yr.) Greek: Hebrew	19	5 yrs.	19	Moral Philosophy

UNIVERSITY COMMON COURSE

19	3rd Class: Natural Philosophy	**GRADUATE IN PHILOSOPHY**
18	(Physics)	(qualification for schoolmasters)
17	2nd Class: Maths (Arith & Geom:	
16	Cosmogony: "Astrology.")	
	1st Class: Dialectic	

COLLEGE

16	**ATTESTATION OF FITNESS**	in every notable town, in-
15	Latin, Greek, Logic	cluding Edinburgh, Glasgow, Old
14	and Rhetoric.	Aberdeen, St. Andrews, Dum-
13	4 yrs.	fries, Jedburgh, Brechin, Argyle,
12	Scholarships, especially for rural	"Channonrie of Ross" (Inver-
	pupils, compulsory attendance for	ness), Kirkwall.
	the really able.	Subject to inspection quarterly by ministers, elders and other well-educated townsmen.

GRAMMAR SCHOOL

12	Grammar and the	in every burgh and in parishes
11	"Latin Toung." (4 yrs.)	able to find a suitably qualified
10	Compulsory attendance for all	master.
9	those able to profit.	
8		

ELEMENTARY SCHOOL

8	First Rudiments and	in every parish.
7	Catechism.	
6	Compulsory attendance for all.	

Note. Allowing for obvious differences in curriculum and period of compulsory attendance, this scheme shows some resemblance with that worked out for the Kingdom of Fife by Dr. Douglas McIntosh, and with the general arrangements of American education in that:

(1) All attend primary and junior secondary schools (but the Reformers would not have compelled our "Modified" pupils to attend the latter).

(2) The senior secondary school *follows* from the junior secondary school instead of being parallel with it as is now more usual in this country.

(3) The real work of the Universities is done *after* the first three years.

A P P E N D I X   M

DIAGRAMS ILLUSTRATING THE ORGANISATION OF
THREE TYPICAL BURGH SCHOOLS
WITH RURAL CATCHMENT AREAS

Diagram 1.

THISTLEBURN GRAMMAR SCHOOL
(Primary Department 300 pupils;
Secondary Department 350 pupils.)

AGE	1 (A)	1 (B)	2	3	4	5
		S.IV				
		S.III.B	S.III.C			
	S.II.A	S.II.B	S.II.C	S.II.D		
14	S.I.A. Academic	S.I.B. Technical	S.I.C. Practical	S.I.D. Modified		
13	TRANSFER OR "QUALIFYING" EXAMINATION					
12	P.VII.A	P.VII.B	VII	VII	VII	VII
11	P.VI.A	P.VI.B	VI	VI	VI	VI
						V
10		P.V.	V	V	IV	
9		P.IV.	IV	IV	III	
8		P.III	III	III	II	
					II	
7		P.II	II and I combined	I	I	
6		P.I		II		
5						
	1		2	3	4	5

(Column 5: Single-Teacher School)

This diagram gives a fair picture of the educational arrangements in a small burgh and its surrounding villages and "mains."

School 1 is the burgh omnibus school, with streaming in its top primary classes and a special class for older primary pupils of very low ability. School 2 is a primary school in a fair-sized village, or possibly the Catholic school in the burgh. School 3 could be a typical village school, or the Episcopalian school. In either case P.I, II, III include some pupils of "upper-middle-class" or even "upper-class" background, who will go on to a preparatory school at 8 or 9. There may also be one or two rather able pupils who will join P.VIIA at School 1.

S.III.A does not exist as its potential pupils have moved on to a Senior Secondary School. Some of them have gone to S.IIIB taking the place of S.IIB pupils also transferred to the larger school. S.II.D pupils go on to S.III.C.

S.IV consists of pupils who have not reached the age of 15 at the beginning of what therefore becomes their fourth year in the Secondary Department. Most of them reach that age by Christmas and this class may have no separate existence, being taught along with S.IIIB.

The four secondary streams are labelled A, B, C, D for the sake of convenience, but may easily have other letters or names (e.g. Academical, Technical/Homecraft, Rural, Modified).

204

Diagram 2.

DUNLOCH ACADEMY

(Primary Department 390 pupils;
Secondary Department 400 pupils).

AGE	Ordinary Grade			
	S.IV A/B			
15				
	S.III.A	S.III.B	S.III.C	S.III.D
14				
	S.II A/L	S.II.B	S.II.C	S.II.D
13				
	S.I A/L	S.I.B	S.I.C	S.I.D
12				

TRANSFER OR "QUALIFYING" EXAMINATION

	P.VII.A	P.VII.B	
11			
	P.VI.A	P.VI.B	PRIMARY SCHOOLS VARIOUS
10			
	P.V.A	P.V.B	as shown in preceding diagram.
9			
	P.IV		Some only go as far as
8			P.IV hence the 5th, 6th
	P.III		and 7th primary classes
7			at Dunloch itself, though
	P.II		streamed, are still quite
6			large.
	P.I		
5			

This diagram shows another fairly typical "omnibus" school in a small burgh, fed by Catholic, Episcopal and village schools.

Pupils taking Latin, and others thought likely to achieve success in "Highers" transfer at the end of the second year to a Senior Secondary School. Those aiming at Ordinary Grade only, including some originally placed in the "B" stream, remain in the school up to the end of their fourth year in the Secondary Department.

Others leave as soon as possible after reaching the age of 15.

The secondary classes may have letters or names other than those shown in this diagram.

L. = Latin pupils.

Diagram 3.

SCOTSBURGH HIGH SCHOOL
(1000 pupils).

AGE							Special Class
17		S.VI					
17	S.V.L.	S.V.A.					
16	S.IV.L	S.IV.A¹	S.IV.A²	S.IV.B			
15	S.III.L	S.III.A¹	S.III.A²	S.III.B	S.III.C		
						S.III.D	
14		S.II.L	S.II.A	S.II.B	S.II.C	S.II.D	
13		S.I.L.	S.I.A.	S.I.B.	S.I.C.	S.I.D.	
12					S. PREP.		

SCOTSBURGH PRIMARY SCHOOL
(600 pupils).

AGE	1	2	3	4
			S.I	S. I
			S.II	II
			S.III	III
11	P.VII.A P.VII.B P.VII.C		P.VII A P.VII B	P.VII
10	P.VI.A P.VI.B P.VI.C		P.VI	P.VI
9	P.V.A P.V.B. P.V.C		P.V	P.V
8	P.IV.A P.IV.B	P.IV	P.IV	P.IV
7	P.III divided but not streamed	P.III	P.III	P.III
6	P.II divided but not streamed	P.II	P.II	P.II
5	P.I divided but not streamed	P.I	P.I	P.I

This diagram shows arrangements in a medium-sized burgh (there is legally no such category, all burghs being "small" or "large") of some 20,000 inhabitants with two small burghs, Dunloch and Thistleburn, both having about 4,000 inhabitants.

The main primary school at Scotsburgh (1) is quite separate from the High School and has its own Headmaster. School (2) is situated on an outlying housing estate. At present the older pupils are transferred to school 1. As the housing estate grows,

P.V, VI, VII will be added, first for potentially B stream pupils, with an A stream later. At the same time the main primary school may decrease and lose its C stream.

School (3) is a Catholic "omnibus school" but with C and D pupils only in its secondary department. Middle-class Catholic parents often send their children to the main primary school (1) to improve their chances of transfer into the Latin and Academic streams at the High School.

School (4) is a village primary school with a secondary department consisting of modified (D-stream) pupils only, the others having transferred to the High School. This department is too small to be divided into three years and therefore constitutes a single class taken by a post-war emergency-trained teacher (a former R.S.M.) who is not a graduate but a first-class man for this kind of work.

S. Prep at the High School is a class into which pupils originally enrolled at the age of 5 in April and therefore transferred in April, may be placed for a term.

April-enrolled pupils at Dunloch and Thistleburn transfer to the secondary department two terms early or one term late and these two schools therefore have no preparatory class.

Since the High School is larger than the secondary departments at Dunloch and Thistleburn together, it has, from the start, a stream consisting entirely of pupils who take Latin as well as French.

There are more pupils in the third year than in the second, because academic pupils from Thistleburn and two-language and other highly academic pupils from Dunloch arrive at this stage. Consequently there are two academic streams in addition to the Latin stream. In principle S.A^1 pupils are "non-Latins" who will by-pass "Ordinary Grade" and go straight on to "Highers" at the end of their fifth year. Most S.A^2 pupils will stop at Ordinary Grade (end of fourth year) but some, having done better than expected, will go on to "Highers". Some S.A^1 pupils will take "Ordinary Grade" as a reinsurance.

There are a number of options and some setting in S.IIIA and S.IVA including S.III.L and S.IV.L. Thus History and Geography are alternatives and S.IIIA/L is taken as one for Geography, with a few pupils from each of the three third-year academic forms. History being more popular than Geography, there are two history sets, one consisting of Latin pupils, the other of non-Latins. There are also sets in French and Mathematics.

S.I.B., S.II.B and S.III.B are much larger than appears from the diagram, and "sub-streamed". Pupils in S.I.B^1, S.II.B^1, S.IIIB^1 have a definite career in mind, requiring a certificate in some technical subjects and preferably in English and Elementary Mathematics also. They continue in S.IVB and attempt "Ordinary Grade". Pupils in the B^2 "sub-stream" normally leave at 15 or at the end of their third year and may go into pre-apprenticeship courses. There are also two classes in each year of the C and D streams.

At the other end of the intellectual scale, special arrangements can be made for pupils of such limited ability that they could not even swim comfortably in a "modified" stream.

Scotsburgh High School could be even larger than it is, especially on its "academic" side but many good potential pupils are lost to the fee-paying primary departments of grant-aided schools in Edinburgh, and to preparatory schools in the vicinity. Having entered the independent and grant-aided "systems" at the age of 8 or 9 they continue therein all the way to "A" Level and "Highers" respectively.

BIBLIOGRAPHICAL NOTE

This is the only book length outline of Scottish Education as it stands at the time of writing (March 1962). The historical side, however, is relatively well-documented. Standard works include the following, among others:

Curtis, S. J.: *History of Education in Great Britain,* University Tutorial Press, 1957.

Davie, G. E.: *The Democratic Intellect,* Edinburgh University Press, 1961.

Grant, J.: *History of the Burgh and Parish Schools in Scotland,* Wm. Collins, 1876.

Knox, H. M.: *250 Years of Scottish Education, 1696-1946,* Oliver & Boyd, 1953.

Morgan, A.: *Rise and Progress of Scottish Education,* Oliver & Boyd, 1927.

Strong, J.: *A History of Secondary Education in Scotland,* Clarendon Press, Oxford, 1909.

Curtis and Knox both have useful bibliographies.

Regional accounts include, among others,

Boyd, Wm.: *Education in Ayrshire Through Seven Centuries,* Scottish Council for Research in Education, 1961.

Simpson, I. J.: *Education in Aberdeenshire Before 1872,* (U.L.P.).

The Education (Scotland) Acts from 1872 to 1928 are embodied in

The Law of Education in Scotland, (Wm. Hodge, Edinburgh).

More recent Acts, and the current Schools (Scotland) Code, are available from H.M.S.O., Edinburgh, together with the following among other Scottish Department publications:

Public Education in Scotland, (1958).

Education in Scotland, (Annual Reports published by the S.E.D.).

The Reports of the Advisory Council: *Primary Education* 1946.
                                    Secondary Education 1947.

Transfer from Primary to Secondary Education, 1961.

Also pamphlets on the teaching of most subjects.

O

A catalogue of all S.E.D. publications is available from H.M.S.O., Edinburgh. The Scottish Council for Research in Education also issue a catalogue of their own publications, which include, for instance:

McIntosh, D.: *Promotion from Primary to Secondary Education.*

McLelland, Wm.: *Selection for Secondary Education.*

Committee on Bilingualism: *Gaelic-Speaking Children in Highland Schools.*

For comparison with English, Norwegian and American Education this book should be read in conjunction with:

Dent, H. C.: *The Educational System of England and Wales,* (U.L.P., 1961).

Hove, Olav: *An Outline of Norwegian Education* (Royal Ministry of Church and Education, Oslo, 1958).

Mayer, Martin: *The Schools.* The Bodley Head, 1961. (Originally published in U.S.).

These books are not absolutely comparable.

Director Hove is the administrative head of the system which he describes.* Professor Dent is a private person, albeit highly authoritative, and though his main purpose is descriptive he also makes use of his freedom to criticize. Mr. Mayer and myself are definitely unofficial and our main purpose is to make people think, and eventually act, though we also provide information in the process.

Most Ministries of Education issue printed or duplicated brochures describing the national system, often with the accent on new developments and projected reforms. These brochures, however, are not always available in English. See also my *Schools of Europe* (Bowes & Bowes, 1960: U.S. publishers as for this book: The Canterbury Press, Westminster, Maryland).

* His Scottish counterpart is Sir William Arbuckle, Secretary of the Scottish Education Department.

INDEX

211